Advance praise for

EVERYDAY AMBASSADOR

"We need a cadre of 'everyday ambassadors' to translate our best intentions into pragmatic actions that promote health and social equity. Kate Otto illuminates a way, in our digitized age, to develop deep human relationships to further these goals. Kate's lessons are valuable ones for any young person who, as so many now do, travel in hopes of serving communities far from home."

—**Dr. Paul Farmer**, founding director of Partners in Health and Chair of Global Health and Social Medicine at Harvard Medical School

"Kate Otto's stories illustrate the care, patience, and deep listening that are vital to crafting lasting solutions to social problems around the world. This book shows how humility and perseverance are needed to turn good intentions into meaningful action. It will provide valuable insights for the growing community of globally minded changemakers."

—**David Bornstein**, *New York Times* Opinionator journalist and author of *How to Change the World*

"*Everyday Ambassador* reminds us of the power of human connection, and how courageous self-reflection is a necessary first step for those who hope to responsibly change the world, and be transformed themselves in the process."

—**Gabriel Brodbar**, director of the Catherine B. Reynolds Foundation Program in Social Entrepreneurship

"We live in a world where technology truly can bolster, strengthen, and reinvent people's relationships with our communities, and yet all too often we do not see this happening. Kate Otto proposes a smart game plan, through vibrant storytelling, for twenty-first-century citizenship, and how we can use technology in pursuit of, not deterioration of, strong communities."

—**Trabian Shorters**, vice president of Communities, John S. and James L. Knight Foundation

"Kate Otto gives us an inspiring and clear example of how one must not just exist in the world, but rather be in and of the world. Our world is increasingly interconnected and Kate demonstrates how to embrace that diversity through respectful and responsible global citizenship."

—**John Sexton**, president of New York University

"*Everyday Ambassador* will inspire you to believe in your personal capacity to make a difference. This book reveals the secrets of how to bring people together, even when technology pulls us farther apart. Throughout [Kate's] adventures, she pairs tenacity with humility, revealing a blazingly original voice with which she speaks her mind yet listens deeply to others."

—**Irshad Manji**, founder of the Moral Courage Project

"Kate's focus on humility and international empathy is the type of thinking that will, at scale, solve the most pressing challenges of our time... and it all starts with the individual thinking collectively. If you ever doubted that one person can change the world, read this book."

—**Daniel Epstein**, founder of Unreasonable Institute and Unreasonable Group

"Kate Otto writes as a millennial yet has lessons to offer all of us. She writes from her heart and from her travels and helps us see that 'how' is as important as 'what'; that in order to change the world, we must change ourselves; and finally that deep connections trump multi-tasking. I applaud her commitment and her wisdom."

—**Ellen Schall**, former dean of New York University Robert Wagner School of Public Service

"A necessary read for anyone thinking about contributing to social change. We need informed and honest advocates like Kate to ensure that those seeking to 'help' actually 'serve' and do no harm to our partner communities. Our deepest appreciation to Kate for doing a huge service for community-based development!"

—**Mireille Cronin Mather**, executive director for the Foundation for Sustainable Development

"Kate Otto's stories illustrate how important the contributions of 'everyday people' can be to foreign affairs and international relations in an era of globalization. Her thoughtful assessment of the value of humility and self-reflection is a great read with useful lessons for those of us who make our careers in public service."

—**Andrew Rich**, executive secretary of the Harry S. Truman Scholarship Foundation

"Disparaging [Kate's] generation's addiction to multi-tasking and superficial digital connections, offers hard won critical insights to others who want to be of service in the world as she discovers that the way to change the world is to change yourself."

—**Susan Davis**, coauthor of *Social Entrepreneurship* and founding president/CEO of BRAC USA

"Otto provides encouragement by sharing compelling stories about what she and others have accomplished—both singly and as members of larger organizations. Wise, inspirational, and thoroughly readable."

—***Kirkus Reviews***

EVERYDAY AMBASSADOR

Make a Difference by Connecting in a Disconnected World

KATE OTTO

ATRIA PAPERBACK
New York London Toronto Sydney New Delhi

Hillsboro, Oregon

An Imprint of Simon & Schuster, Inc.
1230 Avenue of the Americas
New York, NY 10020

20827 N.W. Cornell Road, Suite 500
Hillsboro, Oregon 97124-9808
503-531-8700 / 503-531-8773 fax
www.beyondword.com

Managing Editor: Lindsay S. Brown
Editors: Gretchen Stelter, Anna Noak
Copyeditor: Kristin Thiel
Proofreader: Deborah Jayne
Design: Devon Smith
Composition: William H. Brunson Typography Services

First Atria Paperback/Beyond Words trade paperback edition May 2015

Manufactured in the United States of America

10 9 8 7 6 5 4 3

Library of Congress Cataloging-in-Publication Data

Otto, Kate.
Everyday ambassador : make a difference by connecting in a disconnected world / Kate Otto.
pages cm
1. Self-help techniques. 2. Technological innovations—Social aspects. 3. Social change. I. Title.
BF632.O88 2015
158.2—dc23

2014047376

ISBN 978-1-58270-523-1
ISBN 978-1-4767-8677-3 (ebook)

The corporate mission of Beyond Words Publishing, Inc.: *Inspire to Integrity*

What should young people do with their lives today?
Many things, obviously. But the most daring thing
is to create stable communities in which the
terrible disease of loneliness can be cured.

—KURT VONNEGUT

CONTENTS

PREFACE

Tong kosong nyaring bunyinya.
(An empty drum gives a loud sound.)
—Indonesian Proverb

Like so many people, my passion for public service began to blossom at the dawn of a historic social media revolution.

Around the time I started my first high school volunteer gig at an HIV/AIDS shelter in my hometown, the internet had become a standard utility in my household, albeit through a frustratingly unreliable DSL connection. Years later, as I set off on my first volunteer-abroad trip to Mexico, to spend a college spring break at a Guatemalan orphanage, a new social network called Facebook had begun to expand beyond a handful of colleges into my social stratosphere. When I embarked on my sophomore semester abroad in Ghana, YouTube was revolutionizing my ability to share and consume video content online. Upon moving to Tanzania the next summer for an internship, I found Twitter was introducing hashtags into my digital parlance. By the time I arrived in Indonesia after graduate school, digital connectedness had gone global; it was no longer just an American obsession. My friends in Indonesia were more active on social media sites than my peers back home! Facebook friend requests reconnected me to even the rural and low-income communities I had worked with worldwide, where mobile phones had quickly become a staple commodity.

Despite being at the center of this cyclone of connectivity—or perhaps *because* I was so wrapped up in it—it took me several years even to notice the *dis*connectivity paradox into which I had fallen.

My lightbulb moment occurred four years ago on an otherwise ordinary afternoon in Bandung, Indonesia, at the office of Rumah Cemara, an HIV/AIDS center I'd been working with for almost two years. By the rip-roar of Yamaha motorbike engines in the driveway outside, I could tell my coworkers were returning from their morning outreach work visiting our HIV patients at hospitals and on the streets.

HIV had become an issue of second nature to me, as I had remained close with my hometown HIV shelter throughout and well after high school. At the same time, I had become fluent in Bahasa Indonesia and so, in addition to being privy to juicy office gossip and overhearing many an inappropriate joke, I often greeted short-term international volunteers and translated between these English-speaking visitors and my Indonesian coworkers.

On this particular afternoon, twenty travelers were waiting for me in the front lobby. These foreign volunteers were recent secondary school graduates who hailed from nearly every continent and who had a shared idealistic expectation to "change the world." It was a feeling I knew well—the same force that, ten years prior, burst my small-town bubble and pulled me onto the massive stage of social impact work. Looking at their glowing faces, I vividly remembered my own assumptions as a foreigner in a new land. I had assumed that my extra (wo)manpower was hugely appreciated by the organizations I aimed to serve. I had assumed that whatever type of help I offered would be needed and valued. I had assumed that because I believed my help could make a difference, it would.

I learned quickly, however, in my own misadventures and on staff at Rumah Cemara, that foreign volunteers often create more problems than we solve. When people require constant translation services, whether they lack familiarity with a nuanced issue or cannot speak another language, they take time away from local staff, who have important operational duties to attend to. When people don't understand the cultural and historic contexts in which a social ill plays out, their attempts at helping—no matter how well-intentioned—can end up causing more problems. When people have not yet built trust and relationships with those they aim to serve, their help, no matter how enthusiastic, will not be taken seriously.

Throughout ten years of travel, I have gradually grown wise enough to speak less and listen more. What I heard and observed revealed new insights about how I could be most meaningfully involved in social change, and that required developing several new skill sets. I had to drum up the capacity to focus on specific communities and issues—not spread myself thin to the point of barely having an impact anywhere. I needed to cultivate more empathy, since I was seldom able to relate to the painful life experiences of the people I aimed to assist. And I needed far more patience with the slow pace inherent in long-lasting change. Mostly, I needed far more humility—to stop putting myself at the center of a universe I knew so little about. Slowly but surely, the more diligently I practiced these virtues and addressed these obstacles, the more useful I became to the organizations for which I worked.

But the volunteers I faced that day in Indonesia—those I continue to face regularly during my global travels—were as foreign to these values as they were to their new surroundings. I saw in them a reflection of my younger self: low self-awareness and little clarity as to what their roles could and should be in making a difference. Greeting them with the biggest smile I could muster, I gathered them into a circle to inquire politely about what it was they hoped to do with the organization and how we could help one another over the next few weeks.

One student piped up immediately, explaining that they had come to Indonesia through a student exchange program and were sponsored by an international company expecting the students to carry out their annual corporate social responsibility initiative. Or as the student explained, "to do AIDS education in high schools."

My heart sank, pulling my face into a frown that I tried to force upward.

Doing education is not even a viable concept, I thought. Engaging in conversations, facilitating discussions, and developing curricula—*these* are activities that initiate meaningful learning. Yet even if they had been thinking about these activities, Indonesian high schools are not hot spots of HIV. Unlike other parts of the world, in Indonesia the HIV epidemic is highly concentrated among injecting drug users and commercial sex workers. The small percentage of Indonesian high school students engaged in those risky behaviors were likely skipping school anyway, and presumably would be neither interested in nor willing to *do* AIDS education in English, a language they couldn't speak fluently. How could a hasty, one-off, foreign-language education session have any impact? Youth who were at risk for HIV needed just the opposite: long-term, consistent counseling and workshops in their mother tongue. Not one of these visiting students—and clearly not their sponsoring organization either—seemed to realize how ineffective their idea would be.

A worrisome thought crossed my mind: *Beyond wasting the time of local students, might these visitors' misinformation actually make the HIV/AIDS situation worse?* What if a student still struggling with English misunderstood the explanation of risk factors? Would the imposition of foreign guests in a classroom, there only temporarily, make students uncomfortable asking questions about their health?

I stifled my fears and carried on, hoping a silver lining would materialize in the meantime. "What is your timeline?" I asked.

One student explained with excitement, as if they were starring in a reality television series and not dealing with real people's real health and real livelihoods, that they had only three weeks total to implement the task. No consideration had been made—until that moment—for preplanning or postevaluation exercises. What kind of meaningful—or ethical—work could possibly happen in such a short time frame?

Several students also made clear their plans to leave Bandung for a short vacation in Bali before heading home. *Was this just a vacation disguised as a service trip?*

"Your curriculum?" I asked.

They figured they "could Google that part" and seemed unfazed by the fact that not one of them spoke Indonesian. Had they not considered the danger of sharing potentially inaccurate, sensitive health information with local youth in a language they would struggle to understand and feel uncomfortable interacting in? *Although if these volunteers don't know what they're talking about anyway*, I considered, *then maybe it's for the better that they can't speak Indonesian.*

"What is your experience with HIV programs?" I asked, to be sure I was not overlooking any hidden skill sets or holding any misconceptions about the knowledge they brought to the table. But going around the circle again, not a single student could claim any prior public health experience. No exposure at all to the topic of HIV/AIDS, except for one volunteer who spoke with conviction about having debated AIDS drug pricing on her high school's model UN team.

My patience was wearing thin as the afternoon rain began to patter softly on the rooftop. "Do you have any networks within Indonesia already?" I asked. Maybe they had already been introduced to people living with HIV in Indonesia who could provide them with a starting perspective on a topic they were so in the dark about. In a Facebook-fueled era, there were many ways to be in touch with local organizations prior to a volunteer's arrival in a country. But a room full of blank faces signaled that no one had any such contacts, in-country or out.

I felt deeply disheartened. Disappointment fused with my frustration. Exasperation seethed from my every exhale. I wanted them to leave for their Bali vacations three weeks early. I wanted to berate the company funding their misguided initiative for their corporate social irresponsibility. I wanted to chastise their coordinating agency for investing so many resources into a project destined for zero impact.

These international do-gooders were like many I have encountered in the past decade, my younger self included. As if gazing into a mirror, I could recognize these volunteers were falling into the same traps that had once prevented me from making a difference in the world. They demonstrated relative ignorance of a community's true needs and possessed no apparent desire to inquire about them. They planned a short time frame for action, with no vision for the long-term impact of their work. They lacked sufficient energy to see a single goal through, yet possessed an inflated sense of self-importance, overshadowing the needs of those they aimed to serve.

In this moment there could have been a very disappointing ending. But this is in fact where the *Everyday Ambassador* vision began.

It could be argued that these twenty-first-century volunteers are no different from those of generations past. Should we not praise them for simply making the *effort* to extend their horizons and travel abroad? Are they not better than their peers who spend school breaks sleeping in, excessively partying, or endlessly scrolling through Facebook posts and Instagram feeds?

At least these guys are *trying*. Right?

Not quite.

When it comes to making an impact for and within society, intentions alone have always been a weak currency. In a digital age in particular, they become even weaker, as they begin to replace actual, meaningful interactions. Theoretically, we have every tool we need at our fingertips to learn about an issue, gain fluency in a new language, and make connections in far-off places, so that when we do arrive on the scene, we can start building strong relationships from the start. And yet we don't use these tools as often to facilitate strong connections offline, face-to-face, hand-in-hand.

The volunteers I met in Indonesia are not an isolated group. They are accurate representatives of my generation: supremely socially conscious citizens who have everything it takes to change the world—*except* a strong capacity for relationship development, which is the foundation that all social change is enacted upon. For all our endless digital connectivity—constant status updates, perpetual texts, and increasingly hashtagged commentary—we're failing to forge strong in-person relationships. We suffer from a disconnectivity paradox.

Without a doubt, the technical savvy required for navigating an online world is a primary skill set for twenty-first-century citizenship. But in order for these skills to help us be socially conscious everyday ambassadors, we need a very different, albeit complementary, set of values on hand: *focus*, *empathy*, *humility*, and *patience*. These qualities allow us to serve as effective ambassadors in our world of diversity and differing opinions. If we want to leave a positive impact in the places where we serve, we need focus to define specific goals, empathy to find common ground with even our most diverse neighbors, humility to admit we do not always have the right answers but are willing to listen for and pursue them, and patience to see arduous initiatives through to completion.

When I think back to that afternoon with the volunteers in Bandung, I can see how entrenched they were in the common tech traps that can trip us all up. Multitasking often lulls us into thinking through problems, or crafting solutions, in unfocused, choppy ways. Like the volunteers in Indonesia, people desiring to do good in the world are rarely apathetic, but they're also not always *empathetic*: they don't grasp how entrenched an issue is. We don't assess with a critical eye the situation of the people we aim to help, people who can guide us to more effectively reach a stated goal. The online norm of instant gratification fuels us, like the Indonesia volunteers, to (unrealistically) believe significant social change can occur after mere weeks of activities. And the self-centered architecture of our social media accounts leads us, as it did these volunteers, to wax poetic about our own intentions and desires, instead of listening to the people we aspire to help.

So, what was there to be done on that day in Bandung? What are we each to do every day in the face of these dilemmas, whether we're committing these irresponsibilities or we're watching others do so? If our goal is to be a positive force of change in the world, do we pull the plug or keep powering on? Must we abandon our online networks and dive into the real world, becoming digitally detoxed, never to post another update again? Or is digital communication the key ingredient that empowers us to foster immense positive change in the world?

When I think about how to answer these questions, I first think of an interesting declaration that my coworkers at the Indonesian HIV/AIDS center had taped above our office computers. It read: *Teknologi diciptakan untuk membuat hubungan antar manusia menjadi lebih dekat bagi yang berjarak, bukan malah membuat sebuah jarak bagi hubungan manusia yang sudah dekat.* "Technology is meant to foster closer human relationships between those who are far, not create distance between people who are already close."

This call to action—to be an everyday ambassador—is not a simple one. I experienced this complexity on that afternoon in Bandung, when I felt the urge to reprimand the group in front of me. But had I ostracized those young people, I would have been violating the very core lessons of ambassadorship that I have learned over the past ten years: respectful inclusion, honest communication, and forsaking the desire to force my beliefs on others in exchange for building more meaningful—even if more time-consuming—relationships. Trying to reform behaviors you deem as harmful means, at the very least, not employing them yourself.

Or more simply put: changing yourself is the necessary first step to changing the world.

INTRODUCTION

This book is for anyone interested in becoming an everyday ambassador—someone who has not only mastered communications tools of the twenty-first century but learned to use them wisely (including knowing when not to use them), so as to foster meaningful connections with others, whether inside our own communities or halfway around the world. It is for anyone who struggles to carve out time for reflection yet realizes that rushing through life impedes the ability to build relationships. It is for those who know, or at least suspect, that superficial connectivity is interpreted in most other cultures, including earlier generations of Western cultures, as rude, inconsiderate, unengaged, and uninspired. It is for people who want to change the world, whether that means making a difference as close as their hometowns or as far as other countries. Ask a local organization you support what task they really need a volunteer for that you might be able to do. Making stronger human connections doesn't mean that you have to commit to a regular schedule or even large events. It's good enough to simply help neighbors, and organizations, with single tasks that they really need help with, even one-off experiences. Being an everyday ambassador is more about lending a hand, or creating a connection, in focused and specific ways.

This book is the product of relationships and experiences that have inspired me over the past ten years of studying, working, traveling, and serving, at home and abroad, meeting fellow everyday ambassadors on every journey.

Everyday Ambassadors

Whether we venture to other lands or attend to our own neighborhoods and communities, everyday ambassadors are, at the heart, a community of people hungry to see, experience, and feel more genuine relationships. We are always, at first, foreigners, by culture, age, race, religion, or economics, but we take every chance we can to foster stronger bonds that minimize our foreignness and maximize the common ground we share with others. Most important, ambassadors are filled with and fueled by ideas that will change the world for the better.

Everyday ambassadorship is a process that starts from the inside out. Contrary to instant and short-term digital connectivity, it requires sticking to the challenging path of relationship development in order to build long-lasting common ground and, subsequently, common good. It's quite tempting to think that in this age of effortless friending, following, and pinging there could be nothing easier than building new relationships. Yet as you'll read on these pages, we're in the most difficult relationship-building era of all time, and we have to be prepared to work harder at what used to come naturally, to build true connections where artificial ones sprout instantaneously online, distracting us from the three-dimensional humans around us.

For some people, this ambassadorship comes alive through the traditional routes of engaging in study abroad programs and gap-year internships; for others it takes the form of military or Peace Corps assignments; still others circumnavigate the world with international volunteer organizations or expand their horizons through socially entrepreneurial scholarship and fellowship programs.

Yet ambassadorship is just as much alive when we serve and build relationships in our own countries, cities, communities, or even our own homes. More than just dropping off canned goods or silently spooning out mashed potatoes at a soup kitchen on Thanksgiving, everyday ambassadors reach out on a personal level to build relationships with people in their communities who might otherwise be ostracized, stigmatized, or excluded. They are willing to have their horizons expanded by a new experience or relationship. Everyday ambassadors are the people who ask questions before they make assumptions about people to whom they donate goods or time. They are the thoughtful individuals who coordinate fund-raising for friends struggling to pay their medical bills, or the open-minded parents who accept their gay son despite their church guiding them otherwise, or even the observant stranger who offers up a seat on the train to someone who looks exhausted at the end of a long day.

Ambassadorship need not even be an in-person interaction in our digital era; we can use our Facebook statuses to shout out the accomplishments of our friends and family, rather than simply touting our own, or we can stop and comment on a thoughtful blog post or YouTube video with supportive and constructive feedback. Part of what's so special about technology is that it allows people who otherwise cannot travel or be physically active in their communities to still engage and interact with others in meaningful ways. Everyday ambassadors are just as commonly those who give online through meaningful, well-researched donations, write kind and supportive commentary when others share their art online, and contribute deliberately positive, uplifting, and attentive conversations through social media channels.

For every person, at any age, who begins to engage in social impact work, especially when that person is in some way foreign to the beneficiary, everyday ambassadorship suggests there is an opportunity for a positive relationship to blossom—for a seed of understanding to be planted.

What This Book Will Give You

Humans are, by nature, social animals. And so in an era when our options for socialization are increasingly digitized, it's natural that we flock to convenient, reliable, multitaskable forms of communication. The problem is real-life human relationships require something different than digital-profile interactions; real-life relationships are rarely convenient, do not follow a template, and can't be juggled gracefully along with multiple other interactions. We've run head-on into a disconnectivity paradox: becoming so accustomed to communicating in superficial ways online that we are losing our capacity to connect at the deep levels required of meaningful human interaction.

The time has come for us each to take responsibility for our social lives and our social media, to know when to shut down and log off versus when to harness digital technology to connect us to those we otherwise could not reach. The time has come to reconsider the nature of our everyday interactions, whether we're explicitly trying to achieve some social good or whether it's a simple routine engagement. Our disconnection from others and our lack of understanding regarding how our behavior affects others demand that we relearn how to interact: with focus, empathy, humility, and patience.

To become an everyday ambassador, whether it's globally, locally, or within our own homes, we need to integrate these four redemptive qualities into our everyday relationships. After exploring the concepts of the disconnectivity paradox and exactly what an everyday ambassador is, we will spend time with the four characteristics of everyday ambassadorship, redefining what they mean in a digital age and exploring how we can cultivate them at all levels of human interaction.

Throughout this book you will also find stories of notable everyday ambassadors and their trials and triumphs in their own countries and communities, as well as outside of them. The stories of everyday ambassadors in this volume are deliberately diverse—from a community health CEO in Nepal to an education innovator in Kenya to a community organizer in San Francisco. Importantly, the tales of everyday ambassadors in this book are not limited to individuals formally employed in the social impact realm. Just as poignant and inspiring are the vibrant, eye-opening anecdotes of individuals who foster positive changes in their neighborhoods, communities, and households in truly everyday ways.

This book is also full of everyday tips and tricks that will help you make lasting, positive social change even in a highly technologized society. We can—and must—raise the bar on what it means to make an authentic connection in a digitally distracted age. Through a variety of exercises and critical questions, this book will help you cultivate more focus, empathy, humility, and patience, both online and offline.

Through these ambassadors' reflections, everyday examples, and tools that anyone can use in their lives every day and everywhere, *Everyday Ambassador* suggests a set of concrete skills, attitudes, and habits to help aspiring change makers maximize technology's capacity for social change. Changing the world for the better does not mean becoming the next Mother Teresa or Dr. King, after all. It simply means aspiring to learn from others as much as we hope to give back to others and being thoughtful about our day-to-day interactions, whether we work in the social sector or not, whether we're at home or halfway around the world.

THE DISCONNECTIVITY PARADOX

Bechawenyebela, bechawenyemotal.
(He who eats alone, dies alone.)
—Amharic Proverb

This simple yet thought-provoking thesis came as a gentle suggestion from my Ethiopian colleague Asfaw, as we strode the cracked sidewalks of Addis Ababa, Ethiopia, one April afternoon. His scratchy, soft voice announced this ancient Amharic proverb as we walked toward a hidden canteen in the shadow of our enormous office complex, hurrying our pace as gray clouds began to open up above. His adage was a warning as subtle as the sky's.

He who eats alone, dies alone.

Asfaw and I were conducting public-health research together for an international development organization—one of many institutions that design and fund multimillion-dollar programs in health, education, agriculture, and other public services to improve the social and economic well-being of marginalized people. On that particular afternoon, we still had a budget to construct, data collectors to coordinate, and Ministry of Health meetings to plan. His proverb was a polite, indirect criticism of a suggestion I'd made just minutes earlier to eat lunch at our desks. From my perspective, our overdue deliverables and long to-do lists necessitated mealtime multitasking. I was impatient, eager to finish our work, and as someone in the early stages of my career, I wanted to be perceived as efficient, hard-working, and ambitious.

But Asfaw, with the authority and wisdom that came from being twenty years my senior and from a more communal culture than I, refused to take part in my game. He denied me with a polite chuckle and led the way out of our office toward the nearest restaurant.

We settled onto foldout chairs around a small table. He returned to his Amharic wisdom as we peeled off pieces of *njera*, a sour, spongy flatbread, from the platter's edges and used them to grab up the savory beef chunks and sauces spread across the center.

"Do you understand what I mean by that proverb?" he asked me outright, his trilled *r*'s rolling off his tongue as he gestured to the food with one hand and reached for a chunk of *doro wot* with his other. I raised an eyebrow to signal that I had no idea and wanted to hear more; he caught my cue and carried on, snatching another bite. "It's from a story about a man who visits hell."

I leaned on my elbows, inching toward Asfaw to signal my full, unmultitasked attention.

"There in hell, this man finds a table full of starving, suffering souls, even though they sit around a table full of food. They are starving because the only spoons on the table are so, so long." Asfaw exaggerated his words playfully, looking off as if this depressing scene were playing out on the canteen's doorstep. "These spoons are so long they cannot feed themselves! These people are really suffering." He glanced at me again, and I nodded for him to carry on.

"Now. This same man goes on to visit heaven, and he sees almost the same thing: all the people, all the food, all the very, very long spoons. But this crowd is joyful! No one is hungry, and everyone is rejoicing."

I squished up another lump of *njera* but paused before bringing it to my mouth, picturing this juxtaposition of starving demons and full-bellied angels both with torturously long utensils. Asfaw's point became clear to me as he delivered his final words.

"The people in heaven, they used the spoons to feed each other."

Life in the twenty-first century is not so unlike the scene behind Asfaw's ancient proverb. While sharing a meal is a universal manifestation of the joy of interpersonal connection, socialization is a joy now commonly facilitated via digital devices—laptops, smartphones, and phablets—and social networking applications like Facebook, Twitter, Instagram, YouTube, and any method of instant messaging. We humans are becoming limitless in our capacity to connect, and digital communion is becoming as commonplace as daily bread.

But all too often, our tech tools become long-handled spoons, and with no one to help us, we're rendered hell-tethered demons. Rather than technology manifesting social connectedness, it is common that technology ends up shaping our behaviors and habits toward greater isolation. Allowing digital life to interrupt human interaction is now a commonly noted vice: friends seated around a dinner table, each fully engaged in whatever's happening on the glowing screen of his or her smartphone instead of the present, human company; your colleague only partially listening to your conversation because she's sending a text at the same time; nearly colliding with another pedestrian on the street because you're too engrossed in reading an email in the palm of your hand to concentrate on walking courteously.

The ubiquity of mobile and online connectivity and the subsequent diminishing of human connection have become truths of our time. Globally, there are nearly seven billion mobile phone subscriptions[1] (far surpassing the number of humans who have access to a toilet, for reference), and in the United States, over 91 percent of citizens own a mobile phone,[2] a majority of which are smartphones. The Pew Research's Internet Project documented that 73 percent of adult internet users in America used social media sites in 2013, including a whopping 90 percent of eighteen- to twenty-nine-year-olds,[3] skyrocketing from only 8 percent of all users and 9 percent of eighteen- to twenty-nine-year-olds in 2005.

This growth in digital connectivity has not come without consequences to our interpersonal skills. For example, a variety of studies suggest correlations between Facebook use and increased depression and anxiety, particularly among teenagers, prompting the American Academy of Pediatrics to write a full literature review of the topic and create clinical guidelines for physicians to use to factor in social media as a contributor to illness.[4] The Pew Research's Internet Project published a report in 2014 citing predictions about future impacts of disconnectivity, with one expert stating:

> The scale of the interactions possible over the Internet will tempt more and more people into more interactions than they are capable of sustaining, which on average will continue to lead each interaction to be more superficial. . . . The increasing proportion of human interactions mediated by the Internet will continue the trend toward less respect and less integrity in our relations.[5]

These data and predictions force us to confront an eternal question at the forefront of all technological revolutions: Where do we draw the line between using technologies because they meaningfully improve our lives and using them simply because we can?

The convenience of GPS gets us to our offline destinations more efficiently but also eliminates face-to-face interaction when asking someone else for directions. Our addictive, streamlined workflow of linked applications helps us churn out deliverables faster, leaving us more time with family and friends, yet we are a generation marked by jarring ringtones and humming vibrations at the dinner table and on dates—to which we almost immediately respond, abandoning the faces right in front of us and diminishing our capacity simply to be present. Though instant messaging and unlimited updates keep us well-informed, we can become easily swept into the riptide of using technology as a platform for self-promotion instead of community engagement. We can end up feeling persistently impatient, inflexible, and uncomfortable with any length of waiting. We can be conditioned to meet the ever-rising bar of potential for multitasking, engaging less and less with the present moment, and people, around us.

While these negative outcomes are well documented and innately understood, we still struggle to set and keep rules for ourselves, like putting our phones away, on silent, or on airplane mode when in social situations. As a group we've lost (and as individuals maybe never even had) the capacity to give undivided attention and can rarely offer it to even our closest friends and family, never mind the strangers we interact with on a daily basis. Even as technology becomes visibly divisive, obnoxious, and counterproductive, we knowingly continue to feed our digital addictions. Often, the more "connected" we become to millions of digital friends, followers, and fellow social media users, the less in touch we are with our own inner voices and with the people immediately around us.

As referenced in Mark Kingwell's "Beyond the Book" in *Harper's Magazine*, a 2010 study by the University of Michigan found that:

> American college students are 48 percent less empathetic than they were in 1979, with a sharper dip—61 percent—having occurred in the past decade. According to the US National Institutes of Health, the prevalence of narcissistic-personality disorder is nearly three times as high for people in their twenties

as for the generation that is now sixty-five or older. These trends strongly correlate to increasing online connectedness.[6]

It's clear that our online presence and relationships are causing us to lose—or simply never even develop—the sensitivity required to read body language and feel emotional cues—in short, the ability to have real and meaningful interactions with people in front of us. Our minds and hearts are not CPUs. They require time to digest conversations and exchanges that allow us to understand one another (and ourselves). Yet when considering the blurry line between existing online and offline, we tend to crowd out opportunities to log off, shut down, and reboot.

By no means do these dilemmas imply that technology and digital tools are to blame for our diminished interpersonal skills. In fact, it's exactly the opposite. Most technological tools are designed precisely to help us realize the value of shared learning, community contributions, and crowdsourced solutions. The simplest examples include the comfort of sending or receiving an encouraging text message during a difficult life moment or being able to sing "Happy Birthday" to a family member serving or traveling overseas. Beyond the personal, at professional levels, we can move crucial business decisions along at light speed, link any classroom to new worlds of learning, save lives with telemedicine tools, and share or sell our art and music with audiences across continents. Had Asfaw and I met even one decade earlier, we would have struggled to carry out our research together, in the absence of emails, low-cost international calls, and video conferencing. Online interaction and mobile telephony allow us the privilege of engaging with another individual, even half a world apart.

There are even more exciting opportunities that thoughtful digital connectivity presents to people interested and involved in social impact work. Sites like Facebook's Causes.com and Change.org were the first to transform our online landscape by allowing subscribers to raise awareness about issues that matter to them. Since then, many more crowdfunding sites have emerged to help finance social change work, like Kickstarter, GoFundMe, and Indiegogo. The Apple and Google Play stores are now breeding grounds for innovative smartphone apps promoting health, education, and human rights. Sites like Kiva allow us to send donations directly to poor farmers in rural corners of the globe, and sites like DonorsChoose.org allow us to browse the needs of local schoolteachers and directly fund their classrooms. Both types of sites enable us to continue following the progress of the people we serve, enabling meaningful relationships where there would otherwise be no connection.

Using tech tools to change the world is a remarkable effort, and when we use these tools in the right way—to feed each other—we truly see miracles unfold. Take Patrick Meier, who in 2010 was completing his PhD at the Fletcher School when a devastating earthquake struck Haiti, toppling the country's already crumbling infrastructure and killing hundreds of thousands of citizens. The emergency prompted the usual Red Cross call for donations. While this type of giving is certainly genuine and allows us to act on our compassion, Patrick decided to take the concept of authentic connection a full step further; he became a digital humanitarian.

Well before the earthquake hit Haiti, Patrick had already cofounded several organizations addressing humanitarian crises with technology solutions, but Haiti became the first major opportunity to employ his revolutionary concept. He organized hundreds of student and Haitian diaspora volunteers in Boston, and together they used text message and mapping tools to solicit three thousand urgent and actionable text messages from Haiti. These messages located people in distress, in real time, and Patrick shared this data with first-line responders in Haiti to help save hundreds of lives. Above and beyond the idea of acting on compassion with a donation, Patrick pioneered a field in which we can use technology tools to, quite literally, save lives.

But for all the limitless potential we possess for creating real and lasting relationships—and change—with technology, there exists a subtle set of tech traps into which we too often fall, keeping us from using technology for its innately connective purpose.

The Four Tech Traps

The four key tech traps that we may fall victim to on the way to becoming an everyday ambassador prompted the development of the four everyday ambassadorial values—focus, empathy, humility, and patience—to disarm those traps. A first commonly encountered trap is that of multitasking, the deceptive ability to manage a call, a Facebook post, a blog comment, and a final paper all in a simultaneous array of browser and application windows. We think we're being more efficient, killing multiple birds with a single, digital stone, yet leading social science research on the topic shows that multitasking actually makes us *less* efficient.[7] What's more, when it comes to human interaction, we slowly become conditioned to being less present for the people with whom we interact.

A second common trap is becoming narrow-minded, or polarized, in our opinions. While the endless exposure to information on the internet suggests that digital addiction would be the best possible way to build empathy with others' points of view, the application-based worlds that dictate our social lives—Facebook, Twitter, Instagram—ask us to "follow" specific viewpoints and people, and we often end up choosing those who represent, not challenge, our existing viewpoints. Additionally, search engine algorithms are geared to feed us results, and of course ads, that reflect things we've already searched for and talk about regularly, not different views or opinions. What happens when we then try to engage with people whose views we may oppose? If YouTube comments are any judge of our newly conditioned psyches, then the future of everyday diplomacy does not look so bright.

Third, we also need to be aware of the obstacle of self-centered, haughty thinking, which comes naturally in a world in which all of our apps revolve around our personal schedules, and we can become experts in any topic with some basic search engine skills. Having a host of applications perpetually at our service can subtly tempt us to believe that humans around us surely must cater to our needs as well. The tendency to think that we can, with search engines on our side, already know the answer to most any question in the world does not translate well to the terms of individual relationship management, where this omniscience is almost never attainable.

Fourth and last, impatience is a common tech trap, and seemingly unavoidable in a world where our weather forecasts, driving directions, and song requests are seconds away and at our fingertips. If we're not careful, we begin to expect such unrealistic immediacy from the people around us who, unlike machines, cannot give us information or answers at the click of a button. This can be destructive to maintaining the relationships that matter most to us in life and can also render it nearly impossible to get to know people whose lives are incredibly different from our own.

To avoid these four tech traps—distraction, polarization, self-centeredness, and impatience—we have to work on cultivating our focus, empathy, humility, and patience. We need to overcome the disconnectivity that grows so easily when we're focused on our devices and digital networks, instead of on each other as human beings.

An everyday ambassador is precisely the kind of person who has mastered these four skills, and uses them to transform good intentions into positive actions through strong relationships. Everyday ambassadors are not digitally detoxed—they actually use technology regularly and wisely in ways that bring distant people close together, rather than creating distances between people already close by.

This is no easy feat in a world in which human interaction is becoming increasingly more digitized with every passing moment. We'll only move further in the direction of digital disconnectivity, as the prices of phones and tablets plummet and the variety of applications enabling quick connections skyrockets. This will appear to us, at first, as a revolutionary era of connectedness, in which we can access anyone at any time from any place. But when we look closer and examine the now mainstream cultures of multitasking, polarization, self-centeredness, and impatience that dictate life in our digital environments, we realize the ways in which we are drifting apart from one another, failing to make authentic connections.

Thus, everyday ambassadors are those who confront the disconnectivity paradox by honoring human connections in their everyday lives, no matter where in the world they operate. They do so by employing crucial connective skills—focus, empathy, humility, and patience—in everyday interactions, and they tend to approach social problems with an open mind and active listening, instead of proclaiming themselves as saviors or silver bullets. Everyday ambassadors escape the disconnectivity paradox by serving as excellent relationship managers, whether connections are forged online or offline, with or without the support of digital connections. The roads they travel could be cross-continental journeys, racking up passport stamps and foreign phrases, or they could be explorations of the backstreets and Main Streets of their own communities.

The common tie between all everyday ambassadors, no matter how far they travel, is seeing human connection as a two-way street, in asking in every new interaction, *What am I providing, and what do I need in return?* Many times we may find ourselves giving in dollars and cents, buildings and equipment, medicines and materials, time and effort. And we will likely find ourselves receiving in the intangible currencies of strength and perseverance, ingenuity and innovation, wisdom and patience, inspiration and passion.

There's certainly no foreign-exchange counter to commoditize these treasures. But there is the transformative concept of feeding each other that Asfaw so powerfully suggested. And this is the mark of an everyday ambassador: a person who can calculate the trade internally, listening intently to what is being requested, and staying awake to all that is received in return.

WHAT IS AN EVERYDAY AMBASSADOR?

Before you speak ask yourself: Is it kind, is it necessary, it is true, does it improve upon the silence?

—Shirdi Sai Baba

As the disconnectivity paradox reveals, the degradation of our interpersonal relationship management skills comes not from technology itself but from our individual choices about how—and how often—we allow technology to overtake our social interactions. To overcome this, our creativity in using tech tools to build bridges and connect socially must be matched with the wisdom to disconnect when we need to focus on offline environments. This means not only learning to identify our digital comfort zones—the cherished constant refresh of an Instagram feed, the reassurance of accumulating Facebook likes, the expectation of pushed alerts and responses—but also deliberately defying them.

We must regain, or build anew, our capacity for thoughtful, undistracted human interaction; we must think of ourselves as everyday ambassadors. Ambassadors, in this sense, hearken the spirit of diplomatic and cross-cultural communicators, the kind of border crossers who represent their national interests in pursuit of a peaceful world. But rather than representing a nation or specific population, everyday ambassadors stand for a single, simple, powerful idea: that thoughtful human connectivity is the answer to most of our social ills in an increasingly digitized world. Rather than crossing borders of nation-states, everyday ambassadors cross borders of comfort zones, amending the communication lapses that are so prevalent in our environments, both online and offline. This everyday style of ambassadorship represents the ideal of being a human connector in an increasingly digital world, and it promotes the use of technology in ways that honor, preserve, and celebrate our humanity.

Some everyday ambassadors are those who quite literally change the world with their savvy, like Patrick's digital humanitarianism, saving the lives of victims of natural disasters. Yet everyday ambassadorship is just as important in our own homes, neighborhoods, and communities—refraining from looking at our phones while we're out to dinner with friends, organizing coworkers to spend a day at a community garden, dutifully facilitating annual charity fundraisers for a favorite nonprofit. Everyday ambassadors, contrary to the conventional image evoked of wealthy world diplomats who often receive their posts as political favors, do not require passports or plane tickets in order to have an impact in the world. Their qualifications lie instead in the realm of the intangible, immortalized in the sage words of Maya Angelou: "People will never forget how you made them feel."[1]

An everyday ambassador is, quite simply, a bridge builder. A connector of the proverbial dots. An individual willing to transcend not just borders, like gender, nationality, and ethnicity, but the limits of our innermost comfort zones, in order to meaningfully connect and find common ground with others. Everyday ambassadors are willing to rethink, or altogether eliminate, stereotypes of people with whom they have little in common, whether they're friends, family members, or strangers on the street. They honor differences and seek out hidden shared interests. They also help others rethink deep-seated, oftentimes false, assumptions in a gentle, nonjudgmental manner.

Everyday ambassadors strive to make the world a better place, whether globally or locally, and do so with a strong focus on crafting respectful, responsible human relationships. Everyday ambassadors reject terminology like *saving* or *helping* others, and instead phrase relationship building in terms of two-way exchanges and mutual growth, remaining self-aware, flexible, and culturally sensitive in their daily interactions.

The term *everyday ambassador* was coined with respect to the ongoing trend toward social impact work, made easier by modern digital technology, including study abroad programs, religious missions, gap-year internships, and scholarship and fellowship programs. The term also speaks to the ever-diversifying demography of nearly all nation-states, as a result of immigration and globalization, and applies to people who build bridges between diverse communities within their own countries, cities, or neighborhoods. Whether we operate locally or globally, diversity increases the likelihood that different viewpoints might clash and creates more need for mediators who see shared values beneath superficial differences. The solutions to our world's most intractable problems, as well as preventing more problems from emerging, require some serious ambassadorial skill sets.

Being an everyday ambassador is not so much a title as it is a way of life. Yes, being an everyday ambassador can mean fighting HIV/AIDS in Indonesia with an informed and humble approach. But it also means kindly addressing your morning barista by name, not taking out your bad mood on an unsuspecting bus driver, or replacing passive-aggressive behavior with peaceful, honest conversations at home and in the workplace. You might be surprised that the smallest efforts can make the most enormous difference.

Opportunities for everyday ambassadorship exist all around us. They are abundant anytime we travel abroad, like learning local languages and customs in advance, in order to show respect for the communities into which we hope to integrate. We can even modify our vocabularies to show more consideration for other cultures. For example, travelers often use the term *Third World country* to describe a nation in which many people remain impoverished, where the travelers feel compelled to visit and to "help." Yet this term, understandably, is somewhat insulting to a person from that country, as there exists an underlying implication that *third* means lesser or of a lower class. (Interestingly, this now common association between economics and numerically categorized countries is misplaced; such ordering originated during the Cold War, when Third World countries distinguished themselves as peaceful and politically neutral, refusing to side with Western NATO First World Allies or with the Communist Second World Bloc.) Replacing this derogatory phrasing with other terms—like *the Global South*, identifying nations south of the equator, or *a developing economy*—makes no implied social judgments about people living in that country and gets us started off on a kinder first note.

We can also be more careful with the language we use to describe the work we hope to achieve in a new place, so as not to belittle or disempower those we aspire to serve. For example, I might feel intimidated if a group of foreigners descended on my city sporting bright, matching T-shirts and proclaiming, "Save North America!" And so I imagine that Kenyans or Ghanaians feel the same if a group of volunteers, no matter how compassionate or well-intentioned, arrive at airports proclaiming their roles as continental saviors instead of their desire to be partners, or just friends! Oftentimes we're genuinely unaware of the message our daily language might send to others, and so even these slight modifications in personal word choice can make a world of a difference.

Being an everyday ambassador is also crucially important in our own cities and communities, where exclusionary attitudes, about everything from religion and gender to socioeconomic status, race, and lifestyle, often still prevail. Prime examples of everyday ambassadors at the local level are the people who spoke up, online and in person, to defend Cheerio's 2013 commercial featuring an interracial couple after it received racist commentary online. Or the small-town South Carolinians who held support vigils for their local police chief, who happened to be a lesbian, after her homophobic boss fired her in 2014. They are the Freedom Fighters of America's civil rights movement, as well as the protestors of all races who put their lives on the line to fight racism in the wake of Trayvon Martin's and Mike Brown's fatal shootings.

Everyday ambassadors are just as equally the people who invest their time in non-life-threatening initiatives, like mentoring, tutoring, or providing technical support to social organizations. They are the countless individuals who facilitate conversations at kitchen tables, in church halls, and on doorsteps, encouraging their peers to see past stereotypes and be more tolerant, accepting, thoughtful neighbors. Everyday ambassadors, whether at an international, national, local, or household level, are the people who embrace differences and see all people as equals, unconditionally worthy of respect.

Being an Everyday Ambassador

Four particular tenets of everyday ambassadorship are set forth in this book—focus, empathy, humility, and patience—but they are by no means the only important values of someone eager to connect with others. Any practices that train us to be more loving, open-minded, and nonjudgmental fit the definition, while those that push us toward discrimination, elitism, and apathy are generally disqualifiers.

Being everyday ambassadors is not only about stating our values clearly but also about venturing to new destinations and actively sharing our values and learning about others'. Whether the destination is based on latitude and longitude or on the distance between one person's ideology and another's, everyday ambassadors are constantly traversing gaps to build bridges. Not constrained to the idea of international travel, this connective behavior is just as powerful when we make efforts to cross comfort zones within our own social circles and households as well. In our own offices and classrooms, we have opportunities every day to listen to others who may seem quite different than us in order to drop our perceived stereotypes and see them as fellow human beings.

Once we have established our values and traveled to that new destination of either place or thought, we are responsible for bringing new, adopted wisdom back into our original home communities and into our own behaviors so that, over time, we create new understanding and relationships between otherwise disparate communities. Facing reverse culture shock, or getting used to your home environment again after being exposed to an incredibly different way of life, is a tall order for most people, myself included. And it can be difficult to explain your changed perspectives to someone who has not shared in your experience traveling to a new country or befriending people in social groups you grew up exposed to. And yet the compassion, respect, and open-mindedness we bring back from these cross-cultural and bridge-building experiences form the building blocks of a better world. It is imperative, albeit difficult, to the creation of a healthier society that as everyday ambassadors we learn how to translate our experiences and lessons learned into meaningful anecdotes for our loved ones and home communities.

Being everyday ambassadors surpasses a single set of values and goes beyond the act of trekking outside your comfort zone. It means using our values and experiences to encourage our native cultures, even in our own homes, to be more open. For some, this means finding ways to make lessons from a cross-continental voyage relevant to family back home. For others, like parents educating their children (or just as common, children educating their parents), it means translating values, like respect for all people, into actions, like warmly inviting a diversity of guests into the home. Everyday ambassadors embrace people they otherwise may have ostracized and consider friends people who may have otherwise been strangers, or even enemies.

The term *everyday ambassadorship* wouldn't be complete without the crucial qualifier *everyday*. Traditionally, the title of *ambassador* brings to mind diplomats, embassies, and elite circles, a wealth and level of power access that is beyond the reach of most of the world's seven billion citizens. And yet in our increasingly globalized and digitized world, we each hold the power to be an ambassador by interacting with those whose upbringings or life experiences are far different from ours and respecting and connecting with those who challenge our comfort zones or underlying biases.

Again, this need not mean that we must trek the Kalahari to link up with desert Bushmen or climb the slopes of Everest to engage with ethnic Sherpas (although both would be fascinating adventures, no doubt). Everyday ambassadorship can be as simple as a businessman accustomed to male leadership respecting a new female manager, or socially conservative parents embracing their child's interracial marriage, or a Christian community welcoming a Muslim family into the neighborhood. It can happen online as well: a Democratic leader following Republican constituents on Twitter for the purpose of staying in tune with a wide variety of perspectives on certain issues, or a conservative voter not defriending liberal friends on Facebook to incorporate a constant infusion of different perspectives into their daily grind. Everyday ambassadorial behaviors keep our minds aware of how easy it can be to *otherize* and categorize people into stereotypes and help us to realize shared values and unite on common concerns.

The applications of everyday ambassadorship are limitless and encompass all people who build bridges among different communities in the name of understanding, progress, and peace. Whether or not someone uses technology to make these connections is not the question. What we must be more attentive to in our digital age is not whether, but how, we choose to employ technology. Are we using it to become closer to people who are distant from us, physically or emotionally, or are we using it to create new distances between ourselves and those with whom we would otherwise be close? The answer to this question lies in understanding the ways we can make our interactions meaningful, two-way, and hopefully long lasting.

The Roadmap to Becoming an Everyday Ambassador

Becoming an everyday ambassador, or strengthening your already existing intuition for being one, relies on cultivating four virtues—focus, empathy, humility, and patience—during all of your daily interactions, whether digital or analog, momentous or mundane. Though it's relatively effortless to type them onto the page, cultivation of these skills gets very messy in real life. They're not rocket science, but they're also not easily accessible, especially in a world where we're conditioned to socialize in rapid, sound-bite snippets and are constantly being overfed information in a wide variety of emotional ways.

When we think about how digitized our world is becoming, with toddlers proficient in iPad swiping and grandparents turning to Facebook, being an everyday ambassador offers a more urgent skill set than ever before, and so we must find ways to build these values into our lives. Countries and counties and neighborhoods grow more diverse by the day, and everyday ambassadorship is a lifestyle choice both online and offline that embraces diversity and bridges differences. It mimics precisely what the internet sets out to do: form relationships among disparate groups that otherwise would be unlikely to link up. The internet helps solve problems of proximity and access to information, while actual everyday ambassadors bridge the invisible but just-as-distant gaps of social and cultural miscommunication.

At a time when international and domestic affairs remain tense between nations and neighborhoods alike, everyday ambassadors have the unique potential to change public perceptions about misunderstood cultures, correct inaccurate stereotypes, and offer alternatives to the conflicts in which we traditionally engage to solve social problems. The best part? Everyday ambassadors require no formal training; you become one once you choose to respect and connect with others who may be very different from you, whether they live down the street or halfway around the world.

FOCUS: WINDOWS OPEN, DOORS CLOSE

الكلاب تعوي و القافله تسير

Il kilaab ti'awee, wil kifala tiseer

(If you stop every time a dog barks, your road will never end.)

—Arabic Proverb

Focus is a skill too easily tossed aside in a world where we praise the multitasker, where devices with myriad functions are always considered superior, and where the ability to work from anywhere often means we never stop doing so, rendering *workaholic* an uncomfortably admirable superlative. On the surface, it seems as if our multitasking makes us supremely productive, and therefore little about that feels problematic. We marvel at the wonders allowed by our technologized world: sending an email instead of waiting for snail mail, WhatsApping a friend while Skyping with Mom while streaming Netflix, opening endless tabs and windows in a daily quest for information. As technological tools become increasingly integrated into our everyday activities—not only through smartphones and tablets but in wearable technologies and real-time, auto-updating applications—we become socially conditioned to multitask with the same effortlessness that our gadgets demonstrate. And we are conditioned to believe this power to be a blessing, not a curse.

The reality is that when we try to juggle many tasks at once, we often never finish any one of them fully. We talk about doing many things and ultimately do very few, often leaving efforts unfinished or abandoned. We rush through projects to achieve short-term gains at the expense of losing our focus on the bigger picture. In our efforts to be more productive, social, and informed, all at once, we may end up slowing down, running in circles, and becoming more isolated and less informed than we could ever imagine.

Why don't we just stop and take a breather? Why do we keep firing on all engines, even if we can tell we're losing a sense of direction? Enter the fear of missing out (FOMO) that pervades young, as well as adult, mindsets. In small doses, FOMO can be a harmless fixation, even a positive force of motivation. But in excess, it can translate into more dangerous outcomes. Dr. John Grohol, a specialist in psychology and mental health, writes about our fixation with multiple, simultaneous digital connections, "It's not 'interruption,' it's connection. But wait a minute . . . it's not really 'connection' either. It's the *potential* for simply a *different* connection. It may be better, it may be worse—we just don't know until we check."[1] And check we do, again and again, without pause for reflection, to the detriment of authentic connection.

The result of multitasking on our everyday relationships is that we become only superficially committed to one another. The palpable social pressure governing our online communities often pushes us to abandon difficulty, rather than stick with tough tasks. We've become so accustomed to shutting down or logging off during information overloads that rather than adopting more moderate workloads, we continue to keep countless browser windows open until it's time to reboot. As these norms begin to infiltrate our behaviors offline, they create very real distractions. Can you recall the last time you kept up an in-person conversation or worked through an assignment without pausing to check your phone? How do we even begin to cultivate habits like focus, persistence, and discipline against the ever-present expectation that we can multitask through our every action?

Simply enough, we start with ourselves. Daniel Goleman, author of *Focus: The Hidden Driver of Excellence*, explained, "The real message is because attention is under siege more than it has ever been in human history, we have more distractions than ever before, we have to be more focused on cultivating the skills of attention."[2] When we think about improving our overall success at work, in school, and in our relationships, focus is tantamount. "The more you can concentrate the better you'll do on anything, because whatever talent you have, you can't apply it if you are distracted." Think about the flight instruction to put on your own oxygen mask before helping others: if we can't focus enough in our own lives, on our work tasks or our relationships in our own homes, then we'll never be able to focus long enough to be of service to others.

One of the most well-known studies on concentration looked at children in New Zealand every eight years, until they were thirty-two, measuring their ability to ignore distractions and focus. Unsurprisingly, their aptitude when it came to focusing was the number one predictor of career success, health, and financial success.[3] What it boils down to is focus equals self-control: being able to finish that email before you begin online shopping, or continuing a conversation instead of checking the text message that just buzzed in. Without focus, you cannot reach your personal peak capacity for effectiveness, health, and happiness. And you certainly can't help others reach theirs.

When it comes to social impact work, only someone who is healthy, happy, and focused can build relationships on trust and respect. Self-help gurus and yogis call this quality mindfulness, or simply being aware of what is going on around you. But it can't be attained if you are consumed by what you might be missing out on or if you are overly concerned with hitting a virtual benchmark. (*One hundred likes! Yes!*)

In the midst of my own chronic FOMO-fueled distraction years ago, a beloved boss reached out to me with the proverb of Shiva and Shakti, the divine Hindu couple, which I now think of when trying to stay focused. Upon seeing an impoverished man, Shakti implores Shiva to leave gold in the poor man's path, and Shiva at first resists. ("I cannot give this to him because he is not yet ready to receive it.") Shakti beseeches Shiva again, so he decides to leave a bag of gold in the man's path. But as Shiva predicted, the man steps right past it thinking it is a rock in the road, his mind so busy with his own tribulations that he doesn't see the fortune directly in his path.

How often do we miss things along our paths because we're distracted by other worries and concerns? Focus means being mindful, aware of, and awake to the world around you, and that can be a tall order in a world where we're bombarded with one hundred new hours of YouTube content every *minute* and take in roughly 174 newspapers' worth of information every day.[4] There are a number of ways to start cultivating focus in your everyday life. Some are even showing up as social games in public places, such as friends piling their phones facedown on the table when out for dinner (whoever picks up his or her phone first pays the whole bill!). Here are some simple first steps to finding your focus:

- When you're working online, keep the number of tabs you have open to a smaller number than usual. You don't have to go cold turkey, but if you're typically in the double digits, try cutting it down to below ten. Eight? See what only having four open does.

- When your work doesn't require seeking online references, shut down your browser or disconnect your Wi-Fi altogether. You'd be shocked how eliminating alerts can fuel you to get more work of a higher quality achieved in a shorter period of time.

- The same goes for your phone. If you're not expecting a *truly* important call, turn your phone off or put it on airplane mode the next time you're dining or hanging out with a friend or your family. Silencing notifications will help curb your desire to check your phone and leave you more present in your human interactions.

- On your smartphone's desktop, try minimizing the number of screens you keep active, and the number of applications you keep in easy access. Try to pare your home screen down to the bare essentials, so that you need to click and swipe a few extra times to get that Facebook, Twitter, or Instagram icon. *Out of sight, out of mind* can be a magical mantra.

- When someone is talking, pay attention to whether or not you're actually listening. Are you processing that person's words or already devising what you're going to say in response? (Or are you thinking of checking your email?) In every interaction, attempt to be present, fully. Just sit and listen.

More Focus Now

There's one key word to moving online focus into your offline world: presence. Presence is the ability to be fully engaged in the task at hand, whether it's a conversation with your sibling, sending an email, or crossing the street. At least once a week, try to institute a "presence policy" throughout your day. If you're chatting with your brother, don't answer any text messages or even check your phone. If you're sending an email, don't pick up a call or scroll through your Facebook wall, and if you're walking to work or class, try *literally* just walking—phone tucked away, observing the people and scenes around you, letting any other tasks that come to mind slip away for the moment. You'll be surprised at how much your productivity increases, and how much more connected you feel, when you're truly present.

Employ Your Focus to Make a Difference

After you've begun to really focus in on the very notion of focus, what is the next step? In the world of social impact, staying undistracted is not as easy as you might think. Most of the time, keeping our sights set on a single goal conflicts directly with our innate, boundless desires to make a difference in the world. Usually when we witness hardship or encounter suffering, our natural instinct is an emotional drive to solve the entire problem, not to address only one focused piece of a solution. Our genuine intentions to make a significant, positive difference in someone's life can often leave us in multitask mode, trying to achieve too much but consequently achieving very little at all. And the social media systems in which we operate tend to nurture, instead of challenge, our tendencies to be spread too thin. We append multiple tweets with mulitple hashtags, working from a place of good intention to show support for many issues. But the parameters enforcing brevity prohibit us from focusing on each issue's details.

For example, in 2012 citizens all over the planet rushed to show their support for Pakistani student Malala Yousafzai, who was nearly murdered by Taliban members trying to discourage women's education. Hashtags like #IamMalala (and Malala's own #StrongerThan campaign in 2014) overtook the Twittersphere, shining attention on girls' education and condemning the extremists' horrific violence. Although gender inequity in education has been an issue for thousands of years, with the right timing, the right technology, and the right turn of events, the story of a brave girl in Pakistan spread across the planet, inspiring us and boosting our general social consciousness. This nearly instant, universal awareness and concern for girls' education was an amazing feat, as it prompted financial investments and increased media coverage of the issue, two major forces that help drive significant social change.

However, the buzz of hashtags and petitions has not necessarily translated into immediate action on the ground for girls' education. The "solution" to Malala's ills is in fact quite complex; improving education in impoverished places, for both male and female students, comes with a bevy of intimidating obstacles. Sometimes there are not enough school buildings or material supplies to support all of the students in a region. Even when infrastructure exists, there may be an insufficient supply of trained teachers, or too many teachers who are hired but are chronically absent or underpaid. Even when both buildings and teachers exist, many families may not have the financial resources to provide even modest school fees for their children and, if financially limited, may choose to give preference to boys. (My grandmother was prohibited from going to college because her immigrant father philosophically disagreed with the prospect.) Girls lucky enough to go to school often have to miss an entire week per month when menstruating, because they lack access to sanitary pads or bathrooms at school. And Malala, like many students

FOCUS IN ACTION

When I think about finding focus in the chaotic world of social change, I think of WhyDev.org, Weh Yeoh's global platform for peer support among people across the globe who are making a difference. Yeoh explains that, more than simply allowing people to connect and share stories, WhyDev provides "a way to reduce stress, avoid burnout, and have access to like-minded people who you can bounce ideas off." This is important for keeping focus: as we lend our voices and energies to social causes, we must remember our own development as well.

worldwide, also lives in a conflict zone, meaning that basic concepts of personal safety are obstacles to attaining education.

When we consider all these factors at once, a challenge like ensuring girls have equal access to quality education can feel dizzying and daunting. It takes a very special person, and the unique quality of focus, to choose just one of these puzzle pieces and try to deconstruct and find solutions to it. What instead happens too frequently, in digital environments especially, is that issues are simplified to hashtagged campaign statements (#girlseducation), which do not give nuance to the variety of small-scale strategies necessary for social change. It's up to an everyday ambassador to choose one strategy, or one locale, to zoom in and focus efforts on—the school buildings, the training and remuneration of teachers, the provision of female hygiene products—and as a result of this undeterred focus, a meaningful, tangible result will blossom.

Overenthusiasm for a pressing social issue is understandable and a natural side effect of the excitement that comes from mastering knowledge about a previously unrealized truth. Instinctually, we yearn to share our new awakening during our first exposure to an issue: the first time we volunteer at a shelter for domestically abused women, the first time we help build a Habitat for Humanity home, the first time we mentor or tutor a local student. Newfound passion for fighting any type of social injustice is commendable! It really is. But translating initial emotions into meaningful actions actually demands that we pull back a little before taking action. By toning down our powerful energy for all we *aspire* to do, we can begin visualizing the small, specific initiatives that we surely *can* do to make a difference.

One of my favorite examples of this undistracted focus, and the benefits it yields, is the story of Mark Arnoldy and Possible, a nongovernmental healthcare organization serving some of the world's poorest patients in rural Nepal. In 2012, on the night of his annual board of directors meeting, with an orchestra of bleating car horns and humming holiday foot traffic echoing up to his office window from New York City's Union Square below, Mark's mind was still in the quiet, verdant hills of rural Nepal, where he had just been on a regular site visit. As he prepared to face his donors and public relations professionals who had leveraged their powers to support his organization, Possible, Mark reflected on his recent travel to the developing country where 25 percent of citizens live below the national poverty line.

In particular, he thought about the unforgiving, thirty-six-hour-long bus ride required to travel from the capital, Kathmandu, to his organization's headquarters in a remote, poor, far-western region. Most of Possible's supporters had never even been to Nepal, never mind the rural hospital where their investments were saving lives every day, yet Mark's board was coming together with enthusiastic commitment to a different kind of journey: ensuring health as a human right for even the world's most disadvantaged citizens.

"It's not self-righteousness or even moral compulsion that pushes us to work this way," Mark said, speaking of Possible's model of providing intensive healthcare to each and every single patient in their catchment area—and by that, he means 1.2 million Nepalis, most of whom have never been provided professional healthcare in their entire lives. "Our model is sensible; it's logical," he noted. "Our team, partners, and supporters share the same level of commitment to our patients as the patients and their families feel for themselves."

Although Mark's compassion is both common practice and common sense, many professionals in the wider international development community criticize organizations like Possible for their acute focus on individual care. With a planet full of people in need, their argument goes, it is unreasonable to invest great wealth into an incredibly hard-to-reach location and a relatively small number of patients with complicated health conditions. Possible's approach is considered too costly, yielding an insufficient return on investment compared to the resources devoted. They diplomatically label Mark's work as "place-based public health," implying that it is inherently neither scalable beyond rural Nepal nor sustainable in the long run.

But so far, Mark's progress in one single community has been remarkable. In the year 2013 alone, Possible fully electrified a local hospital campus with 48 solar panels, funded a surgical center and microbiology lab, grew the hospital's Nepali staff to over 160 members, oversaw almost 500 ambulance referrals, and treated over 34,000 patients. In 2014, that figure grew to over 56,000 patients cared for by over 270 staff. Possible's long-term devotion to community transformation is evident not only in their strengthening of a local hospital, through a unique public-private partnership with the Nepali government, but also in 14 additional clinics and their hiring and training of 160 community health workers to run a far-reaching community health program for over 37,000 rural patients.

In a world where we're constantly pressured to do more in ever-shorter time periods, Mark and his Possible team are taking a different, highly focused approach worthy of emulation. Rather than focusing only on scaling the organization's numeric impact, purpose sees, and serves, the wide scope of human needs within every patient who enters their doors. "Our model of accompaniment and attention to long-term health of all patients is not self-righteous or blatant disregard for cost. It actually represents the ultimate pragmatism: that people don't get healthy unless you make a remarkable level of commitment," he argued, highlighting the value of focusing on a single goal. "I understand that everybody wants a way to make people healthy in a really cheap way. And I know that our level of commitment is really hard and requires commitment and does, quote unquote, cost a lot of money. But commitment is the only way, if you care about being effective."

Everyday Ways to Be Focused

Mark's leadership at Possible presents an exceptional example of cultivating undistracted focus on a single community in order to make a measurable difference in the world, but you don't need to travel around the world or start an organization to follow in his footsteps. There are many ways you can cultivate focus in your everyday life in ways that will yield a better, healthier, more peaceful world.

Part of Mark's great example is that he doesn't pay heed to his critics; he forges ahead with confidence because he knows himself and his organization at a deep level. Similarly, it is most effective, if not necessary, for you to start your practice of focus from small, daily, digital interactions—like email, social media, and texting—instead of aiming first for big, ambitious plans. Great gains are achieved when you focus on yourself—not the you projected on Facebook or Twitter but the you who emerges when you're silent and unplugged. Try focusing first on your own strengths and weaknesses, dreams and drivers, and then you can be a source of positive change in your everyday, offline human interactions.

To employ focus in our everyday lives, it is important that we don't interpret *focus* too literally, as if only certain jobs or career choices will lead to having a social impact. Contrary to popular belief, it's *not* only the social sector where your focused behavior can make a major difference in the world. Though some people may be wired for a career in health, education, or other obvious social services, many people find their passion in the corporate world, in the fine arts, or in other careers where there isn't always a clear correlation between vocation and making a difference. In fact, sometimes there's a stigma that someone who makes good money can't possibly be doing social good in the world. But *focus* does not mean choosing a specific type of social-good career; focus means finding a sector that fits your personality and then finding ways to give back.

Whenever someone confronts me with this eternal self-versus-society dilemma—"I want to help people, but I also need to make money"—I cite the story of Cesar Francia, a lawyer in New York City who emigrated from Venezuela to the United States during high school. Gay, black, and an immigrant, Cesar has always been an advocate for LGBT issues, racial justice, and immigration reform; he worked hard enough and was smart enough to earn a coveted spot at the NYU School of Law, and even served as an aide to Supreme Court Justice Sonia Sotomayor along the way. Yet Cesar's roots are thick with hardship as well. Born in Caracas to ambitious but underprivileged parents, he was raised in a hilly, urban terrain of slums stacked high into the mountains, in a city with staggering rates of murder and violent crime.

Cesar is deeply committed to bridging the disparate worlds of his inherited humble upbringing and his earned world of privilege. Unlike many of his social justice–oriented law school peers, who came from economically wealthy families, he also had complex family financial obligations. He therefore did not take the stereotypical social change job in public defense law after school; he opted instead for a well-salaried gig at a private law firm. "In many ways, taking this path felt alarming, as if I was getting 'offtrack' with my social commitment," Cesar explained.

FOCUS IN ACTION

When Rebecca Corey traveled to Tanzania, she developed two passions: a desire to make a difference in the community and a love for music from the 1970s Radio Tanzania era, songs that existed only on old, fragile recording technologies. Combining the two, Rebecca began the Tanzania Heritage Project: sharing the music's history and planning for the digitization and preservation of an art form deeply treasured by the community. Archiving years of recorded history is a tedious but meaningful task that would have been impossible had Rebecca not kept a sharp focus on the initiative.

But when we examine Cesar's choice, it's clear that a higher corporate salary doesn't mean he must deviate from his desire to do good. As Cesar noted, simply being a member of multiple minority communities—as a person identifying as LGBT, a person of color, and an immigrant—and succeeding against the odds is a victory for those communities. Cesar also sought out opportunities to work on pro bono projects as part of his larger work portfolio, and giving employees time to work on social issues is now frequently the norm within competitive law, finance, and technology companies. What I love about Cesar's story is that it redefines the idea of a meaningful career; we don't need to fit any specific mold to be an everyday ambassador. Rather, any career in any sector presents us with opportunities every day to pursue a focused path of social impact, if we keep our eyes open for the opportunities.

Similarly, being a focused everyday ambassador happens not only in our careers, but also outside of our workplaces as well, and can be as simple as powering down in the presence of other people or stopping the urge to snap and upload a picture during moments of genuine connection in your daily life. Ask the barista making your coffee how her day is and look her in the eye when she answers. After your coworker shares a detail of his personal life with you, remember to ask him about it the next time you chat. Try turning off everything, television included, at least one night a week for a family, or solo, dinner.

Branching out from your daily one-on-ones, you can also practice focus within your various communites, by integrating more human engagement into whatever you do. Organize a block party simply to create conversation opportunities with your neighbors. Make an effort to introduce yourself to others in your building or on your street. Ask a local organization you support what task they really need a volunteer for that you might be able to do. Making stronger human connections doesn't mean that you have to commit to a regular schedule or even to large events. Just go and do a single thing they really need help with, even one-off experiences, so you feel comfortable focusing and helping in a specific way.

For example, when I was young, my hometown rallied around a family whose child had a life-threatening heart condition, a tragedy even more palpable within the intimacy of our tiny town's borders. Knowing that these parents were racking up burdensome medical bills for treatments, surgery, and testing, and rushing to doctor's appointments unpredictably, many households in the community decided to come together and cook meals for this family. This generosity rotated organically and never turned it into an act of sainthood; it was simply what one neighbor does for another in a difficult time. The small, focused idea that originated from one person had a ripple effect in our whole town and evolved into a hugely positive impact that brought some peace to a family during a time of crisis. This type of compassion can happen just as powerfully in the online world as well. Thanks to Kickstarter and GoFundMe campaigns, we can raise money for terminally ill friends, or we can host Change.org petitions to support neighbors in desperate need of advocacy. Coming together in person is irreplaceably powerful, but uniting communities across the globe via the internet has its own unique potency for positive change.

Such simple acts of solidarity are too often missed in a culture of multitasking, where we're perpetually busy and can't seem to spare extra time for interaction. We might naturally respond to suffering around us by feeling sympathetic and sending condolences, but inevitably, we get distracted by our busy lives and often never end up doing anything for that mourning friend or frazzled parent. Sometimes, if we're really too busy, we may not even be aware of the crises going on in our loved ones' lives and therefore can't provide any support. Think about it: if we constantly appear to be stretched too thin, it becomes uncomfortable for others to ask favors of us or share bad news. We are, or are perceived to be, unavailable to take on burdens, which are actually priceless and precious moments; they are the building blocks of healthy communities, everywhere in the world.

The same type of conflict arises when you partake in a volunteer trip or overseas stint as well: if the trip is just one more accolade tacked onto an endless list of activities, then it becomes more difficult to have a deep and meaningful experience. Any travel or service opportunity deserves extensive preparation and attention, such as taking the time to truly research where you're going, the history of the local community, the status of the issue you're aiming to solve, and the customs and cultural norms of where you're staying. Think about what specific talents you possess and, instead of trying to "end poverty" in an entire village, simply offer your talents and time in a way that is requested by the community. Instead of trying to be everything for everyone, focus on one thing you do well, and do it. That is enough. The best volunteers are those who have some idea of what they're getting into and how they can truly be helpful.

And when you arrive abroad, be sure to focus first on the people around you and your relationships with them, whether they're your peers, your elders, or the kids hanging out on your street. Notice details of their life. Converse to every extent possible, even if you need a translator to help. Explain who you are and what you hope to offer, and graciously accept and ask for feedback and opinions. When you focus on the people around you, and building strong connections with them, you will find that any other dramas or dilemmas that arise can be easily solved with the help of a friend.

A Final Word on Focus

Whether in your mind, in your neighborhood, or across the ocean, there are just as many ways you can focus as there are reasons why you should. Focus is the everyday ambassador's antidote to multitasking pressures and the flagging commitment it perpetuates. This means developing habits to follow through with ambitions—or to simply set realistic goals in the first place. In a world where we communicate in 140-character quips and goofy GIFs, we need to work harder to keep our passion alive for in-depth analysis or, when it comes to human interaction, fully involved conversations.

When you return to your world of refreshing your screens and scrolling through repetitive RSS news feeds, it will require superhuman strength to force yourself to focus on a single item for more than a millisecond. But everyday ambassadors need to have the self-control to prohibit constant updates from becoming distractions that pull us in multiple directions. We can pledge to support or complete a single issue at a time and stop overcommitting ourselves. We can make ourselves personal social media policies, like only retweeting articles we have fully examined, not merely skimmed, to resist being swallowed in a sea of sound bites.

Research already proves that when we multitask, we make ourselves less productive. Experience tells us that distraction causes us to lose sight of the bigger picture. The choice is ours to not succumb to various pressures. As our everyday ambassadors, such as Mark, Cesar, and my hometown neighbors, demonstrate, specificity and focused attention leads to positive social change. Focusing our attention on the people and the services we care for passionately might require us to close a few windows, but that is ultimately the key to opening some of the most important doors.

Cultivating Focus

As technological tools become increasingly integrated into our everyday activities, it is inevitable that we will continue being conditioned to multitask with the same effortlessness that our gadgets demonstrate. We will try to juggle so many tasks that we will never finish any one of them fully. We will leave efforts unfinished or abandoned. We will rush through projects to achieve short-term gains and then lose focus on the bigger picture. Against the ever-present expectation that we will multitask through our every action, how can we possibly cultivate habits of commitment, persistence, and focus?

The three reflection categories below are intended for three different purposes.

Inner reflections are questions you should be asking only yourself, and answering as honestly as possible. Jot your responses down in a journal or contemplate them before you go to bed, while on a run, or in the shower. Inner reflection questions focus on your perceptions of yourself and your understanding of your own relationship with the disconnectivity paradox.

Outer reflections are meant for small group discussion, whether you're part of a book club or just want to ask these questions over the dinner table with family or friends. These questions focus on your perceptions of the communities and society around you, and in discussion with others, you should gain a sense of how your opinion might differ from others' as well.

Action steps are meant to move you from thinking about making a difference to actually doing it—whether that means making transforming behaviors in your own life through healthy digital detox or positively impacting someone else's life by being a more aware, present, and thoughtful companion (an everyday ambassador!). Action steps are meant to challenge you to modify your life and push past your comfort zones in healthy ways that equip you to be the most humanly connected person you can be.

Inner Reflections

- When I'm online, do I keep multiple tabs and applications open at once? Why? Do I honestly think it allows me to be more productive?

- What are some recent examples of my multitasking, both online and offline, and what do I think I gained and lost from them?

- How does social media nurture me to feel distracted? Has it ever disturbed my sensitivity to subtle communicative cues offline?

- What is an example in the past few days of when I missed out on giving someone my undivided attention because I was distracted by another activity. How was I likely perceived by that person, and what consequence might I have incurred as a result of being aloof?

Outer Reflections

- When it comes to your work, have you ever resisted an instinct to multitask and focused on completing individual tasks instead? Was it challenging? What tips or tricks helped you achieve focus?

- Is multitasking a social norm in your work, school, or social community? What about the community in which you're doing service work? How might others interpret your rushed behavior?

- What are some examples of when multitasking may have led you to be unproductive at work or in school?

- Can you think of an example in the past week when you needed someone's attention—at home, school, work, or elsewhere—and they were too distracted to offer it? How did it make you feel?

Action Steps

- What has been your most multitasked moment during the past five days? Think about how much you were trying to achieve and subsequently how successful you were. Make a list for yourself of tasks that you think are fine to multitask and ones that you want to vow you'll start doing solo.

- Ask your friends and family for their best tips on how to be efficient, yet still effective, without having to continually multitask.

- Choose one relationship that, over the next week, you will not allow to become multitasked. When you interact with this person, there should be nothing else on your radar, nothing in your hands, and definitely no replying to digital alerts.

EMPATHY: AVOIDING DIGITAL DIVISIVENESS

Pa pale sa ou pa wè ak pwòp je ou.
(Don't speak on the things you can't see with your own eyes.)
—Haitian Proverb

Empathy, the capacity to feel what another is feeling or to see the world from another's perspective, is a highly elusive quality in our digital age. The universal accessibility of so many social media accounts seem to indicate that our empathy would be automatically *strengthened*. The more we're exposed to diverse opinions from all over the planet, the more sensitive and open-minded we become to understanding others, right? Wikipedia is full of extensive articles on every culture, tradition, religion, and lifestyle we could ever imagine wanting to learn about. YouTube and Twitter provide nearly unrestricted access to experiencing, through images and through conversation, the lives of people we may otherwise know very little about.

Yet when examined under a sociological microscope, empathy ends up being more difficult to foster now than ever before, and it's not because we're any less caring or less willing to get to know someone than we were before. It's rather because our digital environments too easily constrict, not expand, our comfort zones. We can easily unfriend someone on Facebook if that person's political opinions insult us, and we can choose whom to follow on Twitter based on opinions we already agree with (made even easier by automated recommendations of what we "might like"). Subsequently, we curate tunnel-vision information flows, a digital divisiveness that separates us from people whose opinions differ from ours. As a result, our empathy often erodes during daily online interactions, and examples of this degradation abound: the commenters on controversial news articles who attack, insult, and name-call strangers for having opposing views; the hatred spewed on Twitter toward famous people (amusingly read by celebrities in the late-night television skit "Celebrities Read Mean Tweets"); the vitriolic Facebook posts in which opinions are forced outward, giving no room for diverse perspectives to suggest counterpoints for discussion. It becomes easy to forget that there is a living, breathing person behind a post we disagree with—someone sitting at a computer just like we are, three-dimensional and flesh and blood.

As we grow into more homogeneous groups, research suggests we become more polarized as well. In 2011, researchers examined over 250,000 tweets in the six weeks leading up to the 2010 US congressional midterm elections, and concluded that sentiments exchanged online, versus face-to-face, are often more extreme and could "exacerbate the problem of polarization by reinforcing pre-existing political biases.... The fractured nature of political discourse seems to be worsening, and understanding the social and technological dynamics underlying this trend will be essential to attenuating its effect on the public sphere."[1] Related research completed just a year prior, analyzing thirty thousand tweets related to the shooting of the late-term-abortion doctor George Tiller, considered pro-life and pro-choice perspectives, and showed that, on Twitter, "people are exposed to broader viewpoints than they were before but are limited in their ability to engage in meaningful discussion."[2] Despite how exposed we are to diverse opinions on social media platforms, these spaces often become catalysts of polarization rather than a means to build bridges or initiate conversations. Rather than try to imagine how people of different backgrounds are feeling or what they're thinking, we become more strongly committed to our own viewpoint.

As a result, when we eventually step away from our digital profiles and back into offline lives, we may find ourselves with more extreme opinions and less capacity for empathy than before we ever logged on. If we're not careful, the way we treat online interactions—often anonymously, rarely with accountability, at times superficially, and usually without risk—could trickle into our offline lives, causing us to be less considerate and delicate with relationships in person. Think about it. When we click Send, we can easily forget that our recipients are as human as we are. The more we interact with automated accounts and manicured profiles, instead of honest, imperfect people, the less we know about our fellow human beings. And if the limited information we can observe about someone's life online means we lack knowledge of the issues they are enduring, we can't possibly reach out and try to make a difference. Might we soon find ourselves forgetting the humanity of the person next to us on the bus, or faulting our family members for their quite natural imperfections, or failing to ask someone, whose life we know little about, even the most basic questions in order to become acquainted? Allowing ourselves to become polarized can put us on the defensive, and if that becomes our default position, there's little hope for meaningful human connection.

To break out of becoming polarized people, we desperately need to practice empathy in our everyday lives. It is at the heart of our capacity to understand even a very foreign other, whether that is someone from a far-off land or just a different faith, sexual orientation, or set of political beliefs than our own. In some ways, those changes can start in our online world and emanate out; if we wouldn't dare be so disrespectful in person, then we shouldn't do it online either. Recite that comment out loud, to a friend, before you post it, and check for passive-aggressive (or straight up aggressive) language. Or try using your insight into online norms to switch up your offline environment. We know that search engine algorithms churn out ads and up-rank articles that a formula suggests we would like, based on past searches. Beyond regularly clearing our cache (or by using incognito windows), we can also take our fixes offline: break up your habits every now and then in ways that require you to interact with people whose lives and life experiences you don't know well, whether that means walking a different route to work or dining at another lunch locale. By keeping our environments diverse, we simultaneously develop our capacity for empathy and everyday ambassadorship. Rather than marching to the beat of our own habits, which can push us deeper into existing comfort zones, concerns, and mindsets, we can disintegrate the us-versus-them barrier when we healthily develop social circles that both reflect and challenge our personal point of view.

When we reject subconscious stereotypes and take opportunities to forge common ground, we overcome the tech trap of being backed further and further into philosophical corners. When we prepare ourselves to hear divergent opinions, rather than hide or delete a controversial post or conversation, we become ready to construct a mature, empathetic response. What are some simple ways to immediately change your online behavior to cultivate empathy?

- Challenge yourself to follow alternative opinions on Twitter and Facebook. Mix up your digital environment so that you're constantly being exposed to more than just your personal beliefs and views. Pay attention to how it makes you feel to see something you disagree with and find ways to channel and express that feeling without it becoming anger or resentment. Think up respectful retorts that stimulate deeper discussion, rather than dismiss opposing viewpoints.

- Adopt a no-delete policy: if you post it, it's permanent (that's the way it works with the spoken word too). That means taking more seriously not just your words, but the impact you think they will have on others and how they'll make someone else feel. Do your best to say what you mean in the most considerate way possible; it doesn't mean you can or should avoid conflicting opinions, but it means you're far more likely to come to a peaceful solution.

- Be less anonymous. Imagine everyone will know it's you behind that comment or just stop posting anonymously, ever, to a website. If you wouldn't articulate a certain sentiment and tone in person, why would you say it anonymously online?

- Do your best to read between the lines, whether of a short status update or a long tirade. Language and punctuation can be more misleading than body language, but do your best to tease out whether someone might be conveying feelings of upset or disappointment. Got an unusually phrased text from a friend? Call back to see if that person is feeling OK. Never heard back after a charged email chain? Check in to make sure there haven't been any misunderstandings.

- Be accountable for what you say. Rather than post an emotional reply that you never follow up on, ask about the feelings of the person you replied to. Craft opportunities for extended conversation, instead of simply trying to push your opinion. Respond to *others'* points; don't just reinforce yours.

More Empathy Now

Although texts, tweets, and chats can be just as personal and intimate as offline conversations, there's a notably missing element:

the ability to hear and see the person you're engaging with. Next time you're opening up to someone, or that person to you, in writing only, keep in mind Albert Mehrabian's 93 percent rule. This professor emeritus at UCLA did a now famous study that says that when someone is communicating about feelings or attitudes, only 7 percent of the interaction is verbal. The other 93 percent is made up of tone of voice (38 percent) and facial expressions and body language (55 percent). That means in purely text and tweet conversations, we may be missing up to 93 percent of the interaction because we can't see our conversation partners' faces or hear their tones of voice. And if we really can't get someone offline, we can at least try to take what info we do have and consider how we might feel in that situation, as opposed to placing assumptions from our own experiences on that person's words.

Employ Your Empathy to Make a Difference

A large body of evidence to prove how far empathy takes us in our journey to connect with others has been compiled at the University of California, Berkeley's Greater Good Science Center. Their studies show, beautifully, that empathy diminishes inequality and racism, deepens intimacy and relationship satisfaction, resolves conflicts, and leads to better performance by healthcare providers.[3] Additional research shows that more empathy correlates with your likelihood of helping someone in need, even if the act is against your self-interest. In *The Altruistic Personality*, Samuel Oliner and Pearl Oliner looked back in history and found that "people who rescued Jews during the Holocaust had been encouraged at a young age to take the perspectives of others."[4]

In 2010, researchers discovered that in the modern-day workplace, "managers who demonstrate empathy have employees who are sick less often and report greater happiness."[5] Research in school environments and among students shows that empathy leads to less bullying and less aggression between students—not because fewer people are bullies but because more empathetic students are more likely to speak up as bystanders and stop bullying in its tracks.[6] In 2011, one report found that more aggressive cyberbullying behavior was linked to lower levels of empathy, and researchers suggested that "training of empathy skills might be an important tool to decrease cyberbullying."[7]

We know how dangerous it can be to live in a world without empathy, even beyond damage that happens in the schoolyard and in the workplace. In 2013, Australian researchers linked the polarizing environment of different social media platforms with the growth of political extremism. They concluded that "Twitter provides extremist groups with increased opportunities to magnify and heighten the influence of their message. . . . New media influences extremism by reinforcing extremist policy, providing easy access to extremist beliefs and mobilising followers with calls to action."[8] British researchers also studying this topic in 2013 analyzed online behaviors of fifteen convicted terrorists, and analyzed the role online environments played in their radicalization process. Findings demonstrated that the internet provides more opportunities for self-radicalization and for converting others to radical viewpoints, accelerates these radicalization processes, and most importantly, enables radicalization processes without requiring physical contact with terrorists.[9] Again, it's not to say that technology is to blame for bad outcomes—arguably, converting more people, more quickly, to radical viewpoints of love, compassion, and respect would be quite welcome—but rather, we simply need to be aware of and careful about the ways in which technology is used as a tool toward negative realities. It's our job to use the tools at our disposal for building empathy, not creating divisiveness.

Making meaningful connections—both local and global, the kind that lead us to make a difference in the world—requires a deep understanding of where another person is coming from, *not* polarized,

EMPATHY IN ACTION

For a dose of empathy in action, check out Jubilee Project on YouTube. Eric Lu, Jason Lee, and Eddie Lee write, produce, and make freely available inspirational short films designed to galvanize people around social causes—in a very unique way. "It does little to solve an issue by simply feeling bad for a victim, rather than feeling fired up about solving a problem together *with* them," said Eric. "Our team, whatever issue we are working on, aims to create greater solidarity with groups doing great work on the ground."

extremist perspectives. The positive effects of empathetic behavior are vast, far-reaching, and cannot be overstated. Stronger interpersonal relationships foster more productive collaboration, healthier and happier work environments, and more successful problem-solving sessions. Among the empathetic, social variables soar: less depression, more cooperation, less conflict, more prosperity. Changes can even be quantified economically as well. Embracing diversity leads to more prosperous cities, according to David Lubell, the founder and executive director of Welcoming America. Recently he reported to *Forbes*, "A welcoming city is more likely to thrive. . . . A person who is welcoming to another resident shows active empathy—the kind that involves concrete steps on behalf of the 'welcomer' to help make the resident's journey smoother. In this way, the empathy imperative is a powerful economic driver that also makes a city a more vibrant, inclusive, and pleasant place to live."[10] Empathy is a value that minimizes misunderstandings, eliminates assumptions and stereotypes, and paves the ground for incredible social change.

When I want to articulate exactly how empathy can foster social change, I tell the story of Ben Orbach, who was a student of Middle East studies at Johns Hopkins University when he realized his opportunity for everyday ambassadorship. In the summer of 2002, Ben decided to move to Jordan for a yearlong fellowship to improve his Arabic language skills. "It was less than a year after the 9/11 attacks, and I saw Arabic fluency as my key to gaining a true understanding of America's challenges in the Middle East," said Ben, a Jewish-American from Pittsburgh. "By moving to an Arab World country, and speaking with and listening to people in their own language, I saw an opportunity to pursue answers to the questions that plagued so many Americans."

Within his first few weeks of studying at the University of Jordan in Amman that fall, Ben befriended Sundos, a nineteen-year-old woman who wore the *hijab*, or Islamic head covering. "Sundos approached me in the cafeteria that September day and asked for help with her English essay," Ben reflected. "I was struck by her courage. She was not only approaching someone whose language she did not speak with confidence but a foreign man from a country that was viewed with suspicion and resentment due to the possibility of war with Iraq."

Ben and Sundos slowly became friends, trading English tips for Arabic lessons, though mostly talking about school and current events. Eventually Sundos asked Ben for more help, this time on how to operate a computer, something she had never used before. Over the course of several afternoons at one of the university's computer labs, he taught Sundos basics that ranged from double-clicking a mouse to searching the internet. In the process, they learned more about each other's lives and dug past prevalent stereotypes of America vs. the Muslim World.

Although the impetus for his move to Jordan was initially grounded in a desire to improve his language skills, Ben began to discover through his social interactions that he was motivated by something even greater. With every conversation, he realized how much he actually had in common with people who were painted in the American media as being very different from him, or even as enemies of his way of life. Additionally, he started to see in vivid, human detail aspects of life in Jordan that he never could have grasped in the same way prior to his arrival, like the distressing socioeconomic challenges facing young people. For example, many young men his own age wanted to get married but could not find jobs with the living wages necessary to maintain a marriage. Poverty that went unreported in US media hindered them from being able to start an independent life.

As his Arabic fluency improved, Ben began dedicating his days and nights to speaking with anyone who would speak back and listening to anyone who had something to say. "The experience made me feel like an unofficial ambassador; I would sit in coffee shops for hours on end, engaged in discussions about US foreign policy, or everyday life in Jordan, or my life back home in America. Even if we disagreed, these discussions were always respectful."

As any diplomat would do, Ben reported back to his friends and family via long email dispatches, because the more he learned, the more he felt responsible for trying to clarify misperceptions on both sides of this divide. If an American like Ben could see a piece of himself in the lives of people so negatively portrayed by his mainstream media, was there not great potential for creating international waves of understanding and empathy rather than conflict grounded in ignorance? The idea was so compelling to Ben that he reshaped his letters home into an engaging, perceptive travelogue, *Live from Jordan*, hoping to spread his insights to a far broader audience.

At the same time, Ben realized that he was just one person, with one narrative. He felt limited by his discussions in Jordan because, at the end of the day, they were just that: discussions. While they served a helpful purpose in cultivating intercultural respect, the Jordanians he met and came to know still returned home from these conversations to unchanged realities, whether dim employment prospects or an absence of certain basic human rights. Having one-off conversations might have made the people on both sides of the conversation feel good in the moment, but Ben knew they did little to help improve his new friends' struggles.

"There was something powerful about that time in history—in the wake of the 9/11 attacks, on the eve of our war with Iraq," Ben recalled. "I felt like we were at a turning point, as if America's relations with the Muslim World, and the Arab World in particular, had to be more multidimensional than a decision to go to war with Iraq, or the rhetoric of 'you are with us or against us.'" To Ben, such an analysis seemed painfully shortsighted, and soon he began to feel frustrated. "The situation made me feel powerless in my ability to impact macropolicy questions that I felt so strongly about."

Ben's experience with Sundos stuck in his mind as an empowering and hopeful experience. Although it seemed many Middle Easterners felt only anger and disappointment toward US policies in their region and across the Muslim World, Ben began to ask himself, *How could I recruit more Americans to become unofficial ambassadors?* He imagined that placing other Americans in simple volunteer roles like teaching computer literacy or tutoring in English could simultaneously serve to break down sociocultural stereotypes—it would cultivate empathy that so many Americans and Middle Easterners were lacking in the politically polarizing wake of 9/11.

Over the next few years, Ben worked his way to founding and directing America's Unofficial Ambassadors (AUA) as an initiative of Creative Learning, a Washington DC–based, not-for-profit organization. By the close of 2014, AUA will have sent or supported more than seventy-five Americans to volunteer all across the Muslim World, in countries ranging from Morocco to Bangladesh to Indonesia. Unofficial ambassadors teach English in public schools as well as private Islamic schools, build websites and Facebook pages for nongovernmental organizations working in human rights, and run summer camps for children who live in marginalized communities.

A certain truth becomes evident from Ben's experience, clarified through the prism of his many unofficial ambassadors' perceptions: more grassroots-level friendships between non-Muslim Americans and the Muslim World can spark positive change in dispelling stereotypes, cultivating empathy, and promoting human development. As his unofficial ambassadors learn during their time with AUA, their missions are not complete upon passing back through immigration in the United States. Just as powerful as the volunteers' learning process while abroad is the task of translating experiences back home to America via community presentations, blog posts, and dinner table conversations. Being ambassadors back to their hometowns allows AUA volunteers to build understanding, correct misperceptions, and cultivate empathy in their home communities.

"Our unofficial ambassadors don't just represent their communities overseas, but they serve as representatives of the people they met, the partnerships they formed, and the accomplishments they achieved together," Ben explained. "They share the worlds they discovered and the people they befriended, and through that process they help to develop this concept of empathy for those previously considered 'the other.'" Following the spirit and intent of Ben's work, AUA volunteers are asked to strive to cultivate empathy and offer a different picture of America to the world and likewise a different vision of the world to Americans. His work establishes in people a new perspective, like the kind he gleaned from befriending Sundos more than a decade earlier in a university cafeteria in Amman, the kind that encourages reconsideration of stereotypes and reconstruction of international relationships from the ground up.

Everyday Ways to Be Empathetic

It is very easy to pinpoint polarizing perspectives at a global level, such as the deep divide between the West and the Arab and

Muslim Worlds that arose in the wake of 9/11 and sparked Ben's empathy journey, but there are often issues just as divisive within a single nation. In a country like America, for example, the diversity of life experience within a single city zip code can be global in scope, and even people who were born and raised in the same borough might have vastly different perspectives based on family life, socioeconomic situation, or identification with a race, ethnicity, or religion.

One of my favorite examples of confronting and engaging this level of diversity is the work of graduate student Uraidah Hassani. While an undergraduate student in New York City, Uraidah worked in a Brooklyn neighborhood where over 30 percent of the population was living below the poverty line, and one in ten teenage girls became pregnant every year. "When I first signed up to mentor thirteen-year-old girls in Brooklyn, I was not prepared," Uraidah said. She had grown up worrying little about her safety or her future, and the girls she met every day after school faced starkly different realities. How could Uraidah make any difference in these girls' lives if she had no idea where they were coming from? How could her compassion be accepted if she didn't know how to properly communicate it?

Volunteering as a mentor to these teens, Uraidah was responsible for fielding questions about sexual relationships and assault, different kinds of drugs they had been offered or seen used in their living rooms, and about domestic abuse they had witnessed against their female relatives, or experienced themselves. "The experience was eye-opening for me," admitted Uraidah, as their issues were conflicts she had never confronted. Although Uraidah felt isolated and different from the girls at first, over time, and with the sustained commitment of her new sisters, she began to find common ground.

At the most basic level, she, like them, was a young woman. Uraidah knew that teenage girls often need support with emotional management, personal development, and respectful relationships. They need tools to manage the challenges in their lives, instead of just pretending away or ignoring the problems. Additionally, through conversation, Uraidah realized that one of the girls' greatest struggles was a feeling of not belonging to their community, a place where they didn't feel safe or respected. "As someone who is of mixed race and an immigrant background, as well as being a woman of color who moved around a lot as a child, I also often felt like an outsider." The more Uraidah dug into her own identity, the more she saw herself in her Brooklyn girls, and the more she saw ways she could contribute helpfully to their development.

After thinking hard about the principles of empathy and the power of uniting people with common struggles, Uraidah launched the Inspiration Network in 2009 as the first online social network exclusively for women and girls. By 2014, it's grown to include hundreds of members, age thirteen to sixty-five, all around the globe, from the United States to Indonesia, from Kenya to Colombia. "Users employ the network's connectivity to improve their lives and support circles of girls and women in their communities," said Uraidah. For example, a group called Women LEAD uses the Inspiration Network to run an online pen-pal program between young women in Brooklyn and Kathmandu, Nepal. "What we see is that even if, and perhaps especially when, it's across international borders, women communicating with fellow women means educating each other on how to reach their fullest potential."

Uraidah then used the network to build up an organization that connects, inspires, and educates women and girls on a global scale through mentorship programs and social change projects, The Women Worldwide Initiative (TWWI). The in-person mentorship component of TWWI includes both group and one-on-one activities for participating girls and provides weekly sessions on topics such as personal identity, self-esteem, conflict resolution, and planning for the future. TWWI has continued to operate in the Brooklyn neighborhood where Uraidah's learning began, a place where there were no other programs in existence that focused on young women's leadership and mentorship.

Uraidah has described TWWI's mentorships as sister-sister relationships, not teacher-student relationships, identifying a common ground that encourages mentors to learn from their mentees as well. "The goal is not to 'help,' 'change,' or 'save' these girls. We support them and challenge them to discover and fulfill their potential." And that goes for everyone involved in the equation. Uraidah believes the negative societal pressures that her girls face are forces that women of all ages remain susceptible to, and she has built TWWI to be a "beautiful exchange that crosses boundaries of age and circumstance to benefit both women involved in the conversation equally."

Uraidah's story highlights an important point: empathy isn't only a tool to ease tension and build communication between opposition groups; it's also a tool that helps us better understand people we're already motivated to help, whether it's our mentees or our friends and family. She shows us that cultivating empathy doesn't even require traveling to a distant land, and additional empathy-fueled projects show us that you certainly don't need to start an entire organization in order to improve your skill set. For example, the Global Poverty Project runs an initiative called Live Below the Line, challenging participants from Western nations to spend just $1.50 in a single day for everything they need, including food, transportation, and any other daily living expense. (You can imagine how quickly things add up.) Although an initiative like this doesn't end global hunger or eliminate extreme poverty, it reminds someone who has never known poverty or hunger of the stresses and challenges of living in such a dire situation. When we put ourselves in another's shoes like this, we may become more likely to donate, vote, and live in ways that support economic development and the alleviation of poverty.

In a similar challenge, in late 2012, the then mayor of Newark, New Jersey, Cory Booker, engaged in the Supplemental Nutrition Assistance Program (SNAP) Challenge, living off of food stamps for one week (roughly thirty-three dollars). Blogging his entire experience, Booker broke down negative stereotypes of welfare recipients by casting a light on underlying issues that perpetuate food insecurity, disease, and poverty in America. Booker guided his followers, his constituents within Newark and those who followed him on social media from all over the planet, to minimize judgmental attitudes. His very public effort to see where someone is coming from showed us how empathy prepares us to be of greater service to others.

When it comes to putting empathy into action, I like to highlight the inspiring story of an American woman named Robin Emmons. Robin had just left a two-decade career in the corporate sector to search for a career path that felt more meaningful when her schizophrenic brother experienced such severe symptoms that he needed to enter a mental health facility. As Robin compassionately helped her brother through his healing process, she noticed that as his mental health improved, his physical health declined; he nearly became diabetic at the facility because of the processed, sugary foods he was given. A passionate gardener, Robin made a choice that felt natural to her: expand her crops a few rows to grow enough vegetables for her brother and other patients. After regularly receiving her produce, the patients' health markedly improved.

It soon came to Robin's attention that over seventy-two thousand people in her city of Charlotte, North Carolina, (about one in every ten citizens) had no access to fresh produce. This phenomenon, known as living in a food desert, plagues both rural and urban areas across America and hits poor families the hardest. Robin could see firsthand the same thing Mayor Booker's challenge demonstrated: when limited to food stamps, low incomes, and little free time, families often have to choose cheap, mass-produced, highly processed foods instead of fresh fruits and veggies, and their health suffers because of it. But Robin took it a step beyond Mayor Booker; having built up empathy from her brother's struggle, she decided to take action in Charlotte and find healthy solutions for all of her neighbors.

"I really thought it was an injustice," Robin said to CNN in 2013. "Healthy food is a basic human right. I decided to rip up my whole backyard and make it all a garden, and it just kind of snowballed from there."[11] Since founding a nonprofit (Sow Much Good) to address this injustice in 2008, Robin has now produced over twenty-six thousand pounds of chemical-free produce. She donates some to churches and community centers serving low-income families, and also has created a network of farm stands where she sells her produce at about half the cost of organic goods in large supermarkets. Thousands of people who were previously forced to purchase junky, processed foods now have an option for healthy produce.

You might think that it was easy for Robin to go the extra mile to serve her community; her compassion for the cause of healthy food access was very strong because she could empathize based on her family experience. But the truth is cultivating a sense of empathy is only a first step. Most people who develop

EMPATHY IN ACTION

An incredible example of empathy is the ed-tech company Kinvolved, cofounded by a former New York City schoolteacher, Miriam Altman. Miriam often saw students' grades suffer because of frequent absenteeism, so she built a web-based attendance application for teachers to communicate with families via SMS. The results? Students began arriving earlier and behaving better after the program's implementation! The newfound empowerment shared by teachers, parents, and students was thanks to Miriam's ability to connect with, not conflict with, students and parents.

empathy for a cause will agree, "That's terrible! I can relate," but they rarely *do* anything beyond commiserating and offering statements of solidarity. Robin is a remarkable example of someone who evolved her empathy into serving others. As she forges ahead with her new career running Sow Much Good, she continues to transform neighborhoods suffering from food insecurity by empowering others to access healthy foods, and even grow them independently.

There are many ways we can emulate Ben, Uraidah, and Robin in our everyday lives. At the simplest level, you can make a point to ask people if you're understanding them when they explain something to you about their lives that you may not be familiar with, whether it's an emotion, a conflict, or a difficult decision. ("What I hear you saying is ___________; is that correct?") All too often, we are unable to help others because we don't yet understand the root of the problem. Rather than feel compelled to give people automatic advice and consolation when they open up, try just listening. As you make sure you've understood what is being said, pay attention to whether they are asking just for your ear or for your advice.

Another important move that we can all make is to put ourselves in environments of diversity, whether it's on campus or at work or online. Being directly exposed to other people's lives is the best way to broaden our understanding of issues we may never have experienced ourselves. Try out new restaurants or partake in new hobbies that might expose you to people who have different backgrounds and beliefs. It doesn't mean you need to alter or modify your identity or beliefs; rather, it's simply a way to remind yourself that people with different life experiences and personalities may have a lot to add to your understanding of the world.

Along the same lines, challenge yourself to be aware that you have stereotypes of people, particularly judgments based on appearance alone. We all do to some degree—whether it's thinking someone with a tattoo must have a tough demeanor, or someone wearing a headscarf or turban is particularly conservative—and it's helpful to acknowledge it and train ourselves to see all people free from these preconceived notions, without projecting our ideas onto them. The better we get at pinpointing our own subconscious stereotypes, the more opportunity we have to see people for who they really are, not who we imagine them to be.

All of these daily practices matter deeply to a goal of affecting social change, because we can't solve social ills unless we understand them. And accessing that important information requires that we employ empathy and improve our ability to communicate with someone no matter the differences. It's good to remember as well that *empathy always trumps sympathy*. Though witnessing tragedy will naturally and appropriately evoke in us pity for victims, this can often lead us to assuming insulting and likely false characteristics, such as that they are helpless or powerless.

Empathy also helps us find success with conflict resolution, helping others in the ways they want to be helped and making sure we're understanding and being understood by others. Conflicts don't just happen across national borders; they also come up regularly in our daily lives and can escalate out of control if we don't have the empathy that brings calm to a situation. In 2013, a small scuffle between two moviegoers, one whose cell phone screen was still lit up when the movie started, ended in a fatal shooting, showcasing how out of control even the simplest misunderstandings can become.

In most of our daily opportunities to practice empathy, solutions are rarely straightforward or clear. When a fellow passenger on the train yells at you for bumping her, it's probably not because you really disturbed her but because she had a rough day and your nudge was a final irritant that set her off. If we can't sense and be empathetic to someone who is in a bad place, we might take the situation personally and go on to feel bad ourselves, and then spread that feeling to anyone we encounter. It takes empathy to read between the lines of what people say or do, and sometimes a simple smile, or silence, is the most profound and wise answer to a conflict.

A Final Word on Empathy

Empathy won't necessarily result in another person changing a behavior for you, but it's always your best bet for inviting some level of resolution instead of aggression. In some cases, the person irritating you is not just being careless but is actually having a rough time (for example, parents of infants crying in public are likely just as frustrated as you by their inability to calm them down), and in these cases, a little empathy can go a long way. Reaching out to offer any kind of support, solidarity, or an "it's OK" might not solve the problem, but it will defuse tension and stress and create positive support where there otherwise might have been toxic energy.

Empathy is also deeply important in helping others the way they want to be helped. A great example of this is learning how to help loved ones managing pain or disease that we do not struggle with ourselves, especially chronic conditions, disabilities, or mental health challenges. These are plights that the affected person knows intimately and that we may have little to no knowledge about. Our initial instincts are usually either rushing to be supportive ("Tell me everything!") or shying away out of fear that we don't know enough to help. The most helpful response falls in between these two extremes: striving to get a sense of what that person is feeling, not for the purpose of finding the answer (there probably isn't a single one) but for the purpose of being able to exist alongside that person, be present with his pain, and let him know that he is not alone. Empathy doesn't demand that we're issue experts—it commands us to be better listeners and more open-minded accompaniers.

Next time you find yourself in rapid email correspondence mode, think for a moment about the concept of a handwritten note:

we must at some level have an idea of what we want to say and how much space it will take up, and we think about word choice as we put pen to paper for each new sentence. Typing out emails gives us more space to be careless with our words (never mind our spelling and grammar). It gives an illusion of transience, that anything we say can be easily trashed, that nothing we say is inked or permanent, even though it might be received that way. One helpful, empathetic exercise is to pause before writing an email to confirm with yourself the point of that message. Reread it before sending to make sure you've achieved, to your best ability, that message. Of course, empathy goes beyond our digital interactions; even when you're in vocal conversation with a friend or a group, try pausing before you open your mouth to contribute. Think, *What am I trying to communicate, and will the words I'm choosing get me there?* We so rarely stop and think before we speak, but it's an exercise in thoughtfulness that can improve our friendships and work relationships. Otherwise, how can we expect empathy from anyone else if we're not being clear about what it is we're thinking or needing?

Cultivating Empathy

Ideally, in the future, our approach to interacting with others will be fully saturated in empathy: an awareness that we have a lot to learn from others, whether in our quest to provide resources and support to another person or simply to get along better in our everyday environments. But until that day, our human nature still runs in the opposite direction, the side of us so stoked by technology that we do not always see the need for extensive human engagement with others—the side that thinks we can always Google our way out of problems and insist on seeing the world as an audience we need not engage. Successful global change in the future will mean creatively maximizing people's contributions in ways unheard of before technological tools appeared, as well as being aware of our own limitations that no technological tool will ever enhance.

Inner Reflections

When answering the below questions, again, keep in mind that inner reflections are inquires you ask yourself. You can write your answers down in a journal or think about them in bed, on a run, in the shower, or in other places where you can focus. These are all about self-awareness and understanding your own relationship to the particular tech trap of polarized thinking.

- In what ways does my activity on social media encourage me to think (or act as if) the digital universe revolves around me? When I see any information that either disagrees with my beliefs, or makes me upset, how do I handle such situations?

- Does this self-centered perspective ever present itself in my offline life? If so, in what ways? Can I think of any recent examples?

- When it comes to communicating with empathy, how are offline interactions different from those that I have online? Am I more understanding in one environment or the other? Why might that be?

Outer Reflections

When in a small group, whether it's some kind of club or class or casual gatherings of family and friends, you may find these questions are great tools to get you talking about your communities and society. Also, when you share these questions with others, you get a sense of how others might perceive the same topic differently. Outer reflection helps you open your mind to new ideas and perceptions.

- So often when we think about serving others, we are asked to consider "what am I giving?" rather than "what am I learning?" Think about the last time you did a great thing for someone else. What did you receive in return, even if it was intangible? What is a recent example of a time that you thought you were having a positive impact on someone else but in fact benefitted yourself as well?

- Have you ever been in a situation of wanting to help someone but having no idea what that person is going through? What was difficult about that process?

- Have you ever felt a lack of capacity to sit and listen selflessly during a conversation rather than always reframing discussions around your personal best interest? If so, why might that occur? How are listening skills valued in the communities in which you live and work, and how are they crucial to your success?

Action Steps

These questions help you move from thinking to doing—whether that means something you can do immediately in your own life or a way you can make a change in someone else's. Action steps help you change your own behavior and habits, pushing you past your comfort zones in healthy ways, helping you become more connected in meaningful ways.

- Think about a friend, family member, colleague, or classmate whom most people see as fitting a stereotype but whom you know well as a fellow human beyond the stereotype. When others minimize this person in this way, how do you feel? How did this person come to get pegged with that stereotype, and what are ways you can fight that?

- Think about the reason why you want to help others or be involved in world-changing work. Is the reason ever because you feel bad for other people in less fortunate circumstances? Why might this type of us-versus-them, sympathetic thinking compromise your ability to serve others? Jot down some of your solutions for reducing the us-versus-them mentality and increasing a sense of equality and empathy.

- Do you think enough people would still be interested in service work if language and attitude about "saving others" was eliminated and replaced with terms like "working with" and "learning from"? Or do you feel that more people flock to service work because they enjoy the "savior" identity? What do you think about the strategy of "otherizing" the urgent needs of those we aim to serve versus approaching service work with empathy, yearning to see ourselves in others?

HUMILITY: THE UN-GOOGLE-ABLE INSIGHT

Indlela ibuzwa kwabaphambili.
(Seek the path from those who carved it before you.)
—Zulu Proverb

Self-centered thinking has been a human vice since ancient history—the Greek mythology of Narcissus might ring a bell—but we now have more outlets than ever before, including Facebook, Twitter, Instagram, and YouTube, to express our egoism. Status updates are more often self-promotional than self-reflective, and the social architecture of these environments pushes us to boast to one another, as if likes and retweets are the new drivers of natural selection. We constantly judge our own lives against what comes up on our various feeds, worrying with a FOMO-like fury that we need to be "more" and "better"—that what we have is not enough. Our endless array of apps persuade us to believe we have control over every life outcome. (Spoiler alert: we don't!)

To put it in nondigital terms: we lack humility. Humility is a laudable and highly sensible quality, but it is not an easy attribute to emulate in a world where rewards and accolades are often given to the most self-promotional voices, regardless of their impact or true value. The race for recognition only escalates in social circumstances where the scanning of Facebook walls and Twitter feeds for the sake of comparing our lives to others' becomes a common daily ritual. What emerges is our very human desire to measure up to or surpass the accomplishments of others, rather than feel content with our own commitments. In this increasingly distracted world, we have either lost or never developed the instinct to choose happiness over jealousy when faced with the fruits of our friends' labors and what looks to be their fabulous lives. We immediately begin a game of one-upmanship, wanting to compete instead of to congratulate.

Life without humility, as Narcissus learned the hard way, quickly becomes fatal. When we place ourselves above or beyond others, we ultimately isolate ourselves, and miss out on the opportunity to form relationships with others. R. Eric Landrum, of Boise State University, published an analysis of humility in the journal *Psychological Reports* in 2011, stating, "In addition to the humble person's traits of willingness to admit to mistakes, acknowledgement of gaps in knowledge, and so on, other components of the humility scale focus on openness, flexibility, compassion for others, and being smart but knowing that one is not all-knowing."[1] We all know from our personal and professional lives that these are the qualities we look for in our relationships. Even if humility is not encouraged at a societal level, it remains a desirable quality in forming strong bonds and networks. Author Maia Szalavitz went even further in her *Time* article on humility, explaining that humility is not just helpful but essential to survival: "Evolutionary theory suggests that humble people will be more helpful to the group because a trait that involves subsuming one's own needs to those of others is only likely to be preserved in a species in which cooperation is necessary for survival."[2] And for humans, cooperation, not conflict, is certainly a key ingredient to a successful life.

So why can't we have more humility if it's such a universally appreciated value? To some extent, we can blame human nature for our self-centered tendencies, but there are also notable aspects of our online environments that have pushed us away from one another and inward toward self-conscious tendencies. The most prominent is our newfound instant access to information, via search engines like Google, which have come to redefine our means of asking and answering questions, questions that form the basis of relationship development and issue exploration. Once upon a time, when asked a question that you didn't know how to answer, you would have the options of either pausing the conversation for a phone call to a knowledgeable friend, consulting a book on the shelf, or stating the now long-forgotten acknowledgment, "I don't know."

But the new normal of Google-ability (a phenomenon whose ubiquity means most people don't realize they're experiencing it) affects our psyches in troublingly subconscious ways. We can no longer say, with any level of comfort, "I don't know," because even if we don't know, we *can* know—if we just pull out a phone and look it up. Everyone is expected to be a pocket expert, and for all the fun and benefit that can bring to our lives, it can also prove to be a destructive force in our interpersonal relationship skills.

Though it can be difficult to imagine now, there was something special and important about *not* being an expert at everything and having to acknowledge limitations. Namely, being open to asking others for advice and help, and being able to admit shortcomings, uniquely breeds humility. This is not quite the idea of modesty, nor does it require seeing yourself as lower than others. Rather, humility is a powerful interpersonal skill that allows you to have a clear understanding of your place in the bigger picture, to realize that you are as vital and important as all the other pieces and not more or less important. Humility is the skill by which we accurately measure our own strengths and weaknesses, and a humble person is someone as ready to contribute skills as to admit having little to offer a situation except listening and learning.

How can humility survive in a world that demands us to be pocket pundits, that rewards us for having something to say about everything, and that punishes us for not speaking up, even if we have nothing meaningful to add to a conversation? Humility withers and dies in this environment, and it is essential that as everyday ambassadors we find ways to bring back humility into our lives—starting with ways to build it up online:

- Dare to ask questions! When someone posts an article about a controversial topic, whether it's relevant in your own community or on an international stage, and something seems unclear to you, don't be afraid to ask for more explanation before sharing your opinions. Get the full story first! There's certainly a plethora of informational resources available online, but there are also valuable nuggets of insight and wisdom in the experience and perspective of your friends.

- Put someone else in the spotlight *regularly*. Although Facebook seems to be a place to document your own evolution and accolades, make it a point to shout-out friends for their accomplishments as well, both large and small. Did someone just graduate from school, close on a new home, or run a first road race? Tag that person and celebrate; in a digital world, it's often as close to personal outreach as we can get, and it can make a world of a difference to the person on the receiving end.

- Always admit when you've been proven wrong. Did you misstate a fact in a blog post you wrote? Did you assign blame to someone or something, publically, and then realize you were off the mark? Highlight your mistake prominently, not sheepishly or quietly. It may sound like you're putting yourself in a vulnerable position, but in fact, it's the strongest move you can make.

People notice and will take you less seriously—even if they never tell you so—when you make false statements and fail to follow up. To be open and honest about mistakes shows others that you care about being fair and accurate and fosters even more trust in you and your judgment.

- Acknowledge your supporters. If you're going to make a big announcement on social media about an accomplishment, be sure to shout out anyone and everyone who helped you get to that point. It can be really easy in an individual-brand-driven world to be overly concerned about being distinguished. But even the highest accolades will only take you so far if you fail to thank the people who gave you breaks, opportunities, hospitality, and shoulders to cry on.

- Own your expertise but leave room for improvement. You may very well be an expert, if not *the* expert, on a particular topic or subject. Do the world a favor, though, and don't flaunt it. Your work, writing, and example will speak for itself. What doesn't reflect well is a lack of humility, in which you don't leave space for asking new questions and therefore never evolve your expertise. You always have more to learn, even if you wrote the textbook on a particular topic. Be hungry for new perspectives and invite them into your life, especially in your social media communications.

More Humility Now

Humility is not the act of lowering yourself in comparison to others—it's finding your place within the massive constellation of people around you, those in real-life and those you interact with online. To sharpen your humility, get in a habit of the 1:1 answer/question ratio. This means that for every instance you have something to contribute to a conversation or discussion, include at least one question as well. If you're going to share an opinion about education reform, ask your conversation partners what they think. If you've been asked to tutor children from an underserved neighborhood, offer some advice and also inquire about their lives. For all we have to give, there's always more we have to learn. This idea of asking questions may seem obvious, but once you commit to a 1:1 ratio, you'll see how rarely we actually ask others their opinions! You might also find that people gravitate toward you and feel more comfortable trusting you.

Employ Your Humility to Make a Difference

When it comes to the building blocks of ambassadorship—strong interpersonal relationships—humility is the concrete that keeps those blocks stuck together. Social science and psychology research in the past couple of decades has linked humility with traits like generosity, compassion, and even effective leadership skills. Research from Jordan LaBouff at the University of Maine shows a correlation between humility and helpfulness, and his research partner, Wade Rowatt, explained, "Humility is a positive quality with potential benefits. While several factors influence whether people will volunteer to help a fellow human in need, it appears that humble people, on average, are more helpful than individuals who are egotistical or conceited."[3]

Humility also matters for social impact, because there are many things in our everyday lives that we cannot Google, like the feelings and experiences of others. After we become so accustomed to finding answers on an instantaneous, conveniently sorted search engine, it can be difficult to pry ourselves away from this habit. When friends come to us with dilemmas, for example, an impending breakup, we likely feel prompted to give immediate consolation or an answer. Our minds may even go into search engine mode, immediately spouting off various versions of "Ten Tips to Survive a Breakup," even though most often those friends just want us to listen. We've become programmed to think having the answer is the best response, when in reality, the best response can be silence, admitting we have no idea how someone feels, and listening.

A great example of employing humility to make a difference in someone's life is Zimuzor Ugochukwu, an energetic, social justice–oriented young woman who developed extensive community organizing skills while studying at the University of North Carolina, Greensboro. In 2008 Zim further crafted her organizing expertise while supporting then-Senator Obama's campaign for the presidency, and at UNC, Zim was clearly in her comfort zone; she was a leader among peers and could follow a certain set of rules and tools to achieve social impact success: texting, organizing on Facebook, communicating via email. Once she was forced to step outside that comfort zone, Zim realized that if she wanted to be a community leader, she needed to stay open to self-improvement and not rest on her laurels. "The best leaders are those who don't put their expertise before their teachable moments," she said.

Zim's major teachable moment arrived when she took on an organizing project the summer after the election, working with African American clergy members to galvanize the Fillmore neighborhood in San Francisco

HUMILITY IN ACTION

When Julia Rozier worked at Boston-based, nonprofit Found in Translation (FIT), she served low-income, multilingual women by training them to become medical interpreters. As with many professional service roles, Julia was required to refrain from developing personal relationships with her clients, and often had to turn down their kind offers of rides or small gifts. But through extended conversations and thoughtful exchanges, she found nonmaterial ways to show gratitude for their kind offers. "I wanted to show that we're on equal footing as human beings."

to protect housing rights. To her initial dismay, Zim's expertise in communication norms that worked well with her peers was nearly irrelevant in political activism with people who were both older and of a different socioeconomic status. "I arrived with very little legitimacy," Zim reflected. "That really didn't feel great at first. I feel like our instant access to information means we can always be like Watson [the artificially intelligent question-answering computer system], yet there are so many occasions when, quite legitimately, I might not know the answer to a community's problems. And I can't just Google that."

Zim opted to shake off her feelings of helplessness and instead channeled them into the capacity for humility. She first identified what she did know: Fillmore was a historically black, rapidly gentrifying neighborhood, where people were being pushed out by high rents and a wave of wealthier tenants. At the same time, she identified the many things she was not an expert on, and sat down to listen. "Even though I knew a lot about what had happened historically in the Fillmore, and what *should* happen politically, I didn't know much from the community's perspective, so I sat down with each clergy member and asked them to tell me their story." In doing so, Zim witnessed San Francisco's community dynamics of which she was previously unaware—the troublesome but invisible drug trade, persistence of prostitution, significant struggle of caring for the homeless and serving the mentally ill—and was thus able to engage meaningfully with the community.

And in the true two-way style of humility, Zim's deep listening also made her realize that the Fillmore community held as many preconceived perceptions about *her* as she had of them. This prompted Zim to open up in a way she never had been prompted to do with her peer students back on campus. To many community members' surprise, this articulate, college-educated woman had grown up with her single mother in Minnesota, an immigrant who had escaped from an abusive relationship, living between shelters and halfway houses, but ultimately finding opportunities for education. "I had never opened up like that before while organizing, because in past situations I relied on my expertise, not my life experience, to get me by. This job required me to find a different kind of common ground."

By stepping back from the front-and-center position she was supposed to take and making sufficient time to listen to others and share about herself, she managed to build strong relationships with the community in only a few months' time. "Humility isn't about bowing your head or acting feverishly shy in light of your accomplishments. It's about being coachable and teachable," Zim said. "Be a student of everything, even if you're an expert at what you do."

The challenge of taking Zim's attitude toward social change—being willing to listen instead of command in a community where she was expected to make a difference—is that often our jobs *require* us to be experts. Whether a teacher, a healthcare professional, or an accountant, in any work environment, we are expected to arrive with certain qualifications and be ready to demonstrate our expertise: educate a child, heal an illness, or balance a budget. We understandably might feel vulnerable and inadequate or that our job or job prospects are on the line if we don't have the right answers at the right times to problems we're confronted with. And yet it is so often the case that our expertise is challenged: a student with particular behavior issues disrupts the class, a patient has a persistent pain whose origin our best efforts can't pin down, a business transaction presents complex calculations that we have never confronted before. Whether we're at the beginning of a career or well into one, it is inevitable that we experience firsts throughout our professional timeline, and as we grow into our careers, we realize that it's not about attaining an absolute level of expertise; it is, as Zim noted, being eternally teachable, open to learning, and a lifelong student. Being humble.

When we take this lesson to a global scale, Jennifer Lentfer, international development professional and creator of how-matters.org, would argue that the approach of commanding or feigning expertise is misguided and may even backfire. Over the years, she has come to mentor many young people who are stuck in the centralized rigidities of today's foreign aid sector. One interaction in particular represents for her a broader dilemma when it comes to maintaining humility. "A young man came to me once, explaining that he had been frustrated during a work trip to Kenya because he was not yet an expert," she recounted; he felt that he had little to contribute to his team's economic development project because of his junior level. His grievance reflected the fixation on status and title that permeates our professional worlds, a fixation that can become an obsession in a digital world, where it is easier than ever to one-up peers via public-facing profiles.

Such an obsession is no surprise, considering that in today's hypercompetitive work arenas, people are often rewarded for their hard skills, such as research and technical expertise, and not their soft skills, such as listening and facilitation—skills so vital to success. This is understandable and quite necessary in specific technical fields, like performing surgery, flying a plane, or engineering a skyscraper. But for any job that involves a human-facing component—from business to education or government and beyond—there is something precious about thinking beyond subject-area expertise and into the learning that happens when we listen to the people we set out to serve. "In all of the conversations he'd ever had about development in school or at work, he likely was never taught that building relationships based on warmth, vulnerability, and trust could be core determinants of the effectiveness of his work," Jennifer said about the man. For example, although he wasn't yet a PhD level development economist, he could still play a just as (if not more) powerful role in the project in Kenya by developing trusting relationships with people in the low-income communities that would be affected by the project.

Taking a humble approach also means deferring to the real experts—not those who have spent years studying the problem but those who are living in the midst of it and can articulate most powerfully about potential solutions.

Everyday Ways to Be Humble

How do we start building this vulnerability into our work, especially social impact efforts, in a way that doesn't leave us feeling uncomfortably exposed? One key step is to start being a better listener, a seemingly impossible task when we're so constantly surrounded by noise, pings, buzzes, and digital distractions that even physical solitude never feels really quiet. Even if you live in a busy household or with roommates, even if you work in a bustling classroom or business, carve out at least twenty minutes in every day to sit in silence. Give your brain the chance to flex this unique muscle, the ability to be still. Without this, you'll have a hard time being able to listen to another person without getting distracted, and that means you're more likely to revert to the safety mode of spouting off facts and figures and expertise instead of just listening. It's up to you to create these opportunities to practice and strengthen humbleness. And it's worth the effort; many people find that making time for silence helps them not only connect with others better but minimize stress and anxiety in their own lives.

For some people, this healthy silence is achieved during daily meditation; many of the world's most powerful people and successful social change agents are public proponents of meditation, including comedian Jerry Seinfeld, journalist Soledad O'Brien, investment banking giant Ray Dalio, music producer Rick Rubin, media entrepreneur Russell Simmons, and legendary talk show host Oprah Winfrey. For others, reflection is achieved on a daily morning run, in the shower, or with a journal. The key message is to craft and protect this quiet space for yourself, every single day. Deep connectedness with others really requires that you are first connected, authentically, with yourself. It can feel impossible, at times, to resist the temptations of our rapid-response online culture. But you can make this space by logging off more regularly, and for longer periods of time. Notice your own emotions, like when you make judgments of your own worthiness based on your friends' exciting Facebook and Instagram feeds. Give yourself limits within these breeding grounds for discontent, anxiety, and navel-gazing behavior and opt instead for quiet, offline, thoughtful self-reflection.

Mastering solitude improves listening skills, which in turn provides you opportunities to demonstrate a humble attitude. Do instructions given at work seem unclear? Ask again and listen closely as the process is explained, instead of trying to zip through and finish a deliverable. Sometimes we complain about challenges around us without seeing the bigger picture, which includes space for our own self-improvement and growth. Or if a group project isn't going according to plan, instead of checking your planning spreadsheet or indicator list, try to think outside the box and consider influences that may be beyond your control or expectation. Ever feel like your child (or parent) is simply not hearing what you're trying to ask them to do?

HUMILITY IN ACTION

Nadi Kaonga is a researcher and MD/PhD candidate who assesses the impacts of new technologies in health system reform. Nadi is a senior member of work teams despite her relatively young age. While young people have a lot to offer, they can't be effective in making a difference if they're not humble in sharing their knowledge. When Nadi noticed pushback from a team member, she asked him to lead various components of the project. "Within weeks the tone was completely different. That change made him feel more open, more included. It was a wake-up call for us."

Consider that there may be something happening in the bigger scope of their life that you've missed in your specific interactions with them. Usually when our loved ones behave in defiant ways, it's because of influences we may not be witness to. Humility means pushing aside expectations, assumptions, and a desire for control.

When we look at search engines, knowledge-management apps, and wikis, we may consider our access to information as literally limitless, whether the information we seek is historic or happening in real time, in our native tongue or in a foreign language. There is no longer any excuse to not know something or to lack control over an outcome. Consequently, it can feel unacceptable to admit when we do lack knowledge; it can be supremely frustrating to recognize a factor that is out of our control. We can end up feeling defensive in the face of our own ignorance.

When I face feelings of vulnerability in my own life, I often think of the story of Hannah Lane, an American who used to work as a health educator in South Africa, running an entrepreneurship and education initiative for unemployed adults. Hannah has a master's degree in HIV/AIDS and a rich set of experiences in HIV prevention, an indisputable expertise, but upon her first visit to South Africa, she knew she arrived as a stranger to this particular community she was assigned to support. Aware of her place in the bigger picture, Hannah struck an incredible balance between expertise and humility, doing her best with the knowledge she possessed but leaving room to modify her tactics for her new environment.

One important, but not immediately obvious, detail that Hannah noticed about her new home was that her class participants' most pressing concerns were not actually related to HIV; they were related to unemployment, crime, and domestic violence. "Of course, past HIV courses had been so low impact," Hannah reasoned. "There was no tie-in to the participants' most essential interests." She opted to host a series of community forums with local leaders and current project participants in order to modify the HIV curriculum to suit their circumstances. "I was seeking to understand the real barriers this community faced," she explained, outlining how she determined what social changes were most needed, and ended up expanding her workshop from HIV 101 to include issues that were tangential to HIV/AIDS but intimately relevant.

Each week over the next four months, Hannah and her twenty-five program participants gathered at a community center. In the place of lengthy lectures, Hannah offered interactive workshops that invited participants to join in discussions about not only HIV/AIDS but also violence, job skills, family planning, and nutrition. Activities engaged participants in petitioning local police units to conduct community safety exercises, writing letters to political leaders on health and welfare policies, crafting personal nutrition plans, and performing skits to practice communicating with loved ones about sensitive issues. Though many of these lessons were not initially introduced as being related to HIV, the disease nevertheless came up in conversation, organically, every single week.

Retention in Hannah's workshop series was the highest on record in the history of the organization. "What I realized was that I needed to meet people where they're at," Hannah said, attributing her success to having put the ownership for the workshop style and material firmly in the hands of the community; she had considered the community's needs, encouraging them to bring their thoughts, knowledge, and ideas to the table. "By building something together, and jointly crafting solutions, we created something with meaningful, long-lasting impact."

While Hannah's humility is sensible, it is not an easy attribute to emulate. We're constantly battling a very human instinct to compare and contrast, to measure up to or surpass the accomplishments of others. We are also pressured by the expectations we hold of ourselves and our desire to emulate a certain identity. When we fall short of our identity expectations, or those we imagine others have of us, this translates into anxious, navel-gazing behavior, instead of thoughtful self-reflection, and diminishes our capacity to listen to others or acknowledge ourselves as part of a bigger picture.

While Hannah's instinct for humility seems particularly strategic in international settings, it's a skill set that makes just as big a difference when employed within our own hometowns. It's not only important for the explicit success of social entrepreneurs, but also for enhancing our everyday interactions. A timeless example of this is the life of Henry Stelter. In 1941, Henry married his high school sweetheart at the age of twenty-two, and promptly joined the navy. After serving in World War II, he worked for and eventually co-owned a car garage and dealership in Illinois. Shortly after retiring, Henry suffered a stroke that diminished his ability to communicate through speech. This meant he could no longer engage in his part-time post-retirement work—helping the new owners of the garage—so he and his wife moved to Indiana to be near their only child and his family. Shortly after, Henry's wife died, and Henry was left feeling isolated, confused, and no longer useful in society.

But instead of dwelling on self-pity or wondering if he could deal with losing his identity as a working man and husband, Henry realized he still had a gift to give: he signed up to volunteer delivering mail and flowers to patients at a local hospital, people who faced obstacles ever more insurmountable than his. Henry re-established his place in that bigger picture and redefined what a useful life meant to him. He didn't have to own a business like he had before. He didn't even have to be able to communicate through speech. Many people with successful careers, people who owned businesses like Henry, might have thought delivering mail was a menial task that was below them or not suited for their skill sets. But Henry understood what it meant to be a patient and placed himself on a level playing field with the patients he decided to help.

For the next thirteen years, Henry arose every morning and reported to the hospital six days a week to push a cart; hand patients, nurses, and doctors their mail; and give a nod and a smile, receiving heartfelt thank-yous in return (and, when he retired from that service, an award celebrating his more than sixteen thousand hours of service). Henry's example is a guiding light for all of us: no matter our ability, strength, age, or reputation, we can be of useful service to others if we accept we're no better (and no worse) than anyone else. We're never above even the simplest acts of service, and in fact, it's sometimes these simple acts that make the greatest difference in someone else's life.

The digital worlds in which so many of us now live can be exhausting; we're asked to create and continually craft our identities and are often pressured to compete with others for likes and retweets and even to humblebrag, the act of boasting an accomplishment cloaked in self-deprecating language. But as Henry's life demonstrates, it's when we step outside the identities we think we need and connect with each other on a purely human, equal playing field that we are best positioned to be of service to others. Quite often, the solutions that will best solve the world's suffering do not require us to whip out our smartphones to prove we're right about something (or to simply show we have the answer at our fingertips). Often the most powerful role we can play is simply accompanying someone through a struggle, even without words, like Henry.

A Final Word on Humility

Zim, Hannah, and Henry all suggest how we can incorporate a more humble set of social norms into our everyday lives, particularly if we strive to make some kind of social impact as well. This wisdom tends to be the most obvious when we travel far from home to serve others, in places where we have no personal history or local knowledge, and therefore struggle to find "solutions" to problems we have never ourselves experienced. A lack of humility—or teachability—can end up in a waste of resources, time, and energy, and everyday ambassadors have the power to transform traditional norms of foreign aid into initiatives that involve more listening and accompanying than demanding and directing.

The power of humility resonates as well at local levels and permeates deep into our daily lives. Business and leadership literature are rich with affirmations that humble people are more successful negotiators, and negotiation is an element of any human relationship, not just a business transaction. We negotiate with our coworkers, friends, and loved ones every day: we decide where we want to meet, who will take on different roles in a project, how to collectively care for an aging parent or a sick child. When we approach negotiations with humility, we automatically defuse tensions and initiate a discussion in which everyone feels like they're on a level playing field. This is helpful especially in highly emotional decision-making and situations that require true teamwork in coming to a solution together.

When we think about the impact we hope to have in our social circles, it quickly becomes clear that we all serve as important individual components within a larger, more complicated system. Humbling is the realization that none of us will ever be a silver-bullet solution in and of ourselves—we are part of a bigger picture, and our capacity for influence depends entirely on the successes of others around us.

Cultivating Humility

Why does humility remain an uncommon attribute within our digitized generation? We might look to the rapidly advancing power of search engines, wikis, and knowledge-management apps, and consider that our capacity to access information is literally limitless, whether the information we seek is historic or in real time, in our native tongue or in a foreign language. Smartphone technology puts the power in our hands, 24/7, to be in control of almost every aspect of our lives. There is no longer any excuse to not know something, or to lack control over an outcome. But consequently, it can feel unacceptable to admit when we have a lack of knowledge, and supremely frustrating to recognize a factor that is out of our control. The more we can develop a skill set in practicing humility every day, the more we can maximize our time and energy to make our world, and even just our everyday environment, a much better place.

Inner Reflections

Again, these inner reflections are meant to help you consider the obvious, and not so obvious, ways in which you really are affected by the disconnectivity paradox, particularly your susceptibility to the trend of self-centeredness. Writing out your answers to these questions about humility can be helpful as you forge your own path to be an everyday ambassador.

- Humility often requires the ability to admit where we do not have control over a situation, person, or outcome. In my normal daily life, what are some things I am used to being able to control, especially with technology-enabled knowledge? What would my life be like if I suddenly did not have the same tech tools at my disposal and could not control these outcomes? How would it be challenging?

- What are some skill sets, or knowledge bases, that I have mastered by this point in my life? How long has it taken me to become an "expert" in these things? Have my experiences developed because I have formal education and training, or just life experience, or both? Do I think one is more or less important than the other?

- We often use the term *a humbling experience* to qualify moments when we felt less knowledgeable than we thought we were, whether on a technical topic or just an awareness of a bigger world outside our own. What is a recent time when I've felt humbled? How did the experience make me feel?

Outer Reflections

These outer reflections are best discussed in a small group or with at least one other person whom you trust and who will be completely honest with you. When you have a discussion with open-minded, supportive friends, it can be easier to witness and understand new perspectives, and think more critically about the society you live in and the communities you're a part of.

- What is a recent time you wished you could control another person's behavior or reaction to a particular situation. What aspects of the interview were out of your control and why? How did the experience leave you feeling?

- Whether at work, on a service project, or in relationships, what are your tips for finding balance between a desire for good outcomes and the reality that there are simply some situations (such as other people's behavior) that you cannot change?

- Oftentimes the people whom our service projects aim to benefit are not consulted as experts during program design. Why does that happen? How would you ensure it doesn't happen in any future projects you become involved in?

- Sometimes, at a societal level, a strong sense of independence can overshadow the amount of value given to humility. Do you think this unapologetic independence is particular to specific cultures such as American or Western cultures? Or is this present in all societies? In what ways is it helpful to personal development? In what ways is it damaging or dangerous?

Action Steps

As before, these action steps will help you implement the qualities of an everyday ambassador into your everyday life. These range from the first few baby steps we can all make, like powering down devices more often, but there are also steps to help you find and be prepared for volunteering service opportunities.

- Next time you feel afraid to admit you don't know the answer to a question or feel unsure about how to manage a complex situation, resist the temptation to immediately Google an answer. At least once a day, try asking a human being for advice or support first, or better yet, try saying, "I don't know yet."

- At work, at school, or in your current service project, remind yourself of the people you're aiming to serve, whether they are your customers, patients, students, or beneficiaries. Have you consulted them as experts yet? If not, find ways to honor and incorporate their advice into your planning.

- Think about the qualities required to be "teachable"—someone who acknowledges their own imperfection and still strives toward and achieves social change. List a few changes you can make, starting tomorrow, to better enact this balance in your life.

PATIENCE: HIGH SPEED IS NOT HIGH IMPACT

Rawera ringo matek kende owuon,
kod jaduong' gidhi mos to kanyakla gichopo mabor.
(Alone a youth runs fast,
with an elder slow, but together they go far.)

—Luo Proverb

Patience has become an increasingly uncommon trait as we get sucked into a world of instant gratification and immediate updates. Why read a newspaper when we can swiftly scroll through summarized headlines? Why read a full article when we can do a search and zoom in only on the keywords of interest to us? Why trek to the store for a purchase when there's same-day delivery online? Time is valuable, and the apps that populate our smartphone screens empower us to live more conveniently and efficiently, even if, consequently, more impatiently. With our bus schedules, weather reports, taxi requests, and restaurant reviews being so immediately, reliably accessible, it has become unacceptable to have to wait for anything.

But this impatience is not the good kind of impatience that has fueled social change leaders to take urgent and dramatic actions against injustice. It's the draining kind of impatience that diminishes the value of anything noninstantaneous down to *not worth waiting for*. Many digital aficionados treat a slow Wi-Fi connection in a corner café, or being put on hold by a customer service representative as gross human rights violations. Comedian Louis C.K. joked about our society's chronic impatience when he described a flight on which the airline offered Wi-Fi, but when it stopped working, a fellow passenger became immediately frustrated. "How quickly the world owes him something he knew existed only ten seconds ago!" he observed.[1]

Mocking our impatience is funny because it is real, and we see it every day. But beyond our behavior lie serious consequences, including the erosion of interpersonal communication skills and healthy relationships. Technology might work quickly and simply, but human beings notoriously do not. Being impatient waiting for a taxi to appear is one thing, but what happens when we start feeling impatient waiting for a friend's text message reply, a boss's email, or the first like or comment on a Facebook post? If our appreciation for efficiency and speed in technology sinks too deeply into our nature, we run the risk of treating other people with brash, abrasive, or passive-aggressive attitudes, whether it's a customer service representative, a loved one, or ourselves.

Patience is not only a saving grace in relationship management, but it's also a skill that allows us to do better work, even if (or perhaps because) we must work more slowly. In 2013, the Pew Research Center's famed Internet & American Life Project surveyed teachers of students in advanced placement courses, the cream of America's academic crop, and 68 percent of these teachers said digital tools make students more likely to take shortcuts and not put effort into their writing. Almost half of them, 46 percent, claimed these tools make students more likely to "write too fast and be careless."[2] If this is happening with our highest-ranking students, what else might be happening across schools, in workplaces, or in homes?

How did we arrive at this new normal so suddenly? The everyday activities that make up much of our lives have been revolutionized within small time frames, so we have simply moved along with the trend instead of pausing to observe and consider consequences. Not too long ago, professional and academic lives moved at the pace of typewriter-produced documents and hand-crunched numbers—the speed of ink, paper, and simple mechanics. What once took us hours, if not days, software now literally does in seconds. While indisputably efficient, software played an initiatory role in fostering society's instant gratification addiction.

Then came the revolution in personal correspondence. Once a realm of written letters and phone calls, conversations have been reinvented with email and texting. Again, while there are benefits galore of instant communication, our endless options for rewriting, deleting, or editing our thoughts so quickly can also lead us to be less thoughtful with our words and less likely to think about our intentions before verbalizing them. Now, as Facebook and Twitter feeds refresh themselves and multiple communications streams populate our phones, we're in a space in which there is no way to keep up. We are, by definition, always behind, unless we opt out altogether. Understandably, it has become nearly impossible to cultivate patience in such a frenzied, fast-paced world, because society does not reward calmness and restraint. Our new social norms are dominated and pushed forward by survival of the fastest.

The trouble is that efficiency, when defined as exerting minimal effort for maximum benefit, rarely equals effectiveness in real-life relationships. When your best friend went through a traumatic period and you went out of your way to comfort and support her, inconveniencing your schedule in the process, did the peace you brought to her yield any tangible benefit for you? Probably not. Friendship cannot be quantified with any formula, manipulating inputs to predict an expected output. Friendship consists of fulfilling unpredictable and immeasurable expectations that may, besides for the benefits of friendship, negatively impact you: showing up, answering a call, rescheduling a flight, canceling another appointment, sharing your paycheck. Similarly, when we reach outside of our households and immediate friend circles to make a difference in the lives of strangers, the same condition applies: efficiency rarely equals success. If you show up as the new face in a neighborhood or office, down the street or a continent away, trying to accomplish even the most altruistic project will fail if all you focus on is efficiency.

The necessary first steps—simple and intangible—are time-consuming efforts like building trust. But making these investments of time often challenges our addiction to convenience, as we are now trained to abandon anything displeasing with a single click. This makes us poorly equipped to make a difference in the world, whether we're addressing hard-hitting issues like conflict, hunger, and disease or sitting with an inconsolable friend. It is crucial to understand that in most challenging situations, there is no such thing as a fast-track solution. So how do we manage our socially conditioned impulses for quick results while working on problems that demand patient, long-term solutions? These are some quick tricks that you can immediately apply to everyday life:

- Plan time buffers for your day. Be deliberate about not scheduling appointments, meetings, or hangouts back-to-back. Best case, you are able to deal with delays sans stress; worst case, you get to your next stop early or have some free time on your hands.

- Write one letter every week—for whatever reason you see fit, for whomever in your past or present you'd like to reach out to. A short, handwritten letter goes a long way in cementing and bolstering friendships and relationships and forces you to be more thoughtful in the slower-paced process of writing by hand.

- Read at least one full news article per week. Better yet, read two articles, one from a source that is neutral or aligns with your biases and another from a source that presents the issue from the other side. Take your time. Try to understand the issue in a new light, in full nuance.

- Envision the person you're interacting with if you're engaged in a phone or online conversation with a stranger. If you're on hold with customer service, try to remember, before becoming short-tempered, that there's a person on the other end who has been fielding calls all day. If you're offended by a comment you see in an article or post, rather than immediately dismissing that person or firing back an insult, try engaging them in a longer discussion (off the comment board!). Often, when we give each other time and attention, we find we may actually have common ground between our opposing viewpoints.

- Poor Wi-Fi connection? Pages not loading? When you experience moments of slow (or no) internet access, take it as a cue to step back and breathe. Who is around you? What are you sometimes missing in real life when you're moving speedily along online?

More Patience Now

Too often we associate waiting with weakness. If we need to wait for a service or a person, it feels like we're in a vulnerable position, or undergoing a punishment. And yet in reality, the ability to be patient is one of the most powerful positions we can ever embody. In *New York Times* bestseller *Emotional Freedom: Liberate Yourself from Negative Emotions and Transform Your Life*, Judith Orloff suggested a creative exercise to tap into the incredible power of patience: go wait in a long line. Find a line at the grocery store, a shopping mall, a government office, anywhere! And simply wait. "Instead of getting irritated or pushy," suggested Orloff, "which taxes your system with a rush of stress hormones, take a breath. Tell yourself, 'I'm going to wait peacefully and enjoy the pause.'"[3] Practice makes perfect, even when it comes to adopting qualities of calmness and fortitude. Try flexing your patience muscles and finding the power that exists in pressing pause more often.

Employ Your Patience to Make a Difference

There certainly exists a good kind of impatience, the kind that historically has fueled social justice leaders to take urgent and dramatic actions to foster political change, like ACT UP protestors in the 1980s, who got the FDA to expedite approval of lifesaving AIDS medications, or civil rights leaders who demanded equal rights for black Americans.

But there are many more situations in the realms of war, hunger, poverty, and disease in which there are no fast-track solutions. We might feel the inevitable adrenaline rush to which we are already addicted, that of taking quick action in the face of a challenge, but as we foster our determination for social change, we must not move too swiftly, or else we end up burning out and helping no one. After all, as much as we're now conditioned to take quick action to get involved, we move just as quickly toward the exit; it becomes all too easy to abandon that which is displeasing when we're used to being able to double-click an issue off of our screens.

In the realm of social change, patience has manifold benefits. It allows you to create reasonable schedules for projects, and working in a timely way—as opposed to creating an unrealistically fast pace, then failing to deliver—gives you more credibility and allows others to see you as a more reliable person. Managing expectations is a crucial component of any social change work, and patience is the key to achieving it. It also helps to keep in tune with your teammates, who may be working overtime, hearts full of passion. Instituting team break times, to stop and assess progress and solicit crucial feedback, fosters healthy team dynamics.

Globally, you'll also score cultural competence points by living more patiently. In most cultures outside of America and Europe, it is considered wise and sophisticated to be patient and thoughtful, instead of scrambling to meet unrealistic deadlines. Plus, if you're living outside of your home community, for all that you might know about an issue or a place, having the patience to even just read a local newspaper every morning can give you incredible insight on your new environment.

Perhaps the most important thing about patience is that it demands that you consider the person behind the project. Usually when project delays happen, there's a human element to the delay, and that's natural and normal and not worth getting upset about, though we so often do. Try to see that even the most systemic approaches to social change still rely on human emotion and human behavior, which require great patience in order to work successfully. A village will not be cured of a disease overnight. A nation of children will not be enrolled in primary school within a year. Racism and religious

PATIENCE IN ACTION

Through Indego Africa, a social enterprise that links for-profit cooperatives of women artisans in Rwanda with high-end international fashion outlets, Conor French provides his artisan partners with robust business training opportunities, so they don't have to stay with Indego collectives forever. "We want to create effective economic systems within, which our Rwandan partners can employ themselves, even if these take a long time to build up," French explained, a notable departure from today's instant gratification culture.

violence will not stop just because of a very clever and innovative campaign. Inarguably, change takes time. The question is: *Will you stick around to see it through?*

There's one woman I think of often when I describe the beautiful results of patience and sticking around to see a solution through. Toni Maraviglia is an educator and tech start-up founder who, after three years of work with Teach for America in West Harlem and the South Bronx, moved to Muhuru Bay, a rural Kenyan village on the shores of Lake Victoria. Toni moved with a goal similar to the one she had in the United States: to improve access to educational opportunities for Kenya's most remote and underserved students. Specifically, she planned on running a community-based initiative to help students improve their exam scores.

Toni certainly expected a significant change of pace in Muhuru Bay, a place where winding, dirt roads connect scattered settlements of earthen huts and multifamily compounds, where poverty was passed down reluctantly but inevitably to each new generation. But never before had she imagined schools as humble as the ones in which she worked: five grades of children in tattered uniforms combined into a single open-air classroom with a single teacher; desks littering an open yard with pupils scribbling away at math problems beneath an open sky; small bodies seated beneath a massive tree, with spare branches staked out in a circle around them, makeshift walls against which the teacher would tip a poster or blackboard. At first, Toni was eager to get to work, "armed with malaria pills, hand sanitizer, and a data-driven mentality, positive that my efficient, Western ideals would revolutionize a small, impoverished village." And she certainly got some results speedily. She set up a pay-for-performance system that rewarded teachers for students' improved exam scores, and within her first year, she saw passing rates double.

Yet as the months passed, living in a straw-roofed hut with intermittent electricity, staying clean with bucket showers and outdoor latrines, and learning to translate between her Luo-speaking neighbors and the largely English-language material her students were expected to learn, Toni changed her expectations of how fast her small victories could turn into systemic wins. The closer she grew with her students and their families, the more she noticed the subtleties of their dilemma—that is, the inextricable link between access to education and patterns of poverty.

Even though her program had been a success in the schools where it was implemented, the majority of Muhuru students lacked the resources necessary to prepare adequately for national exams. Toni learned that six million of Kenya's nine million primary school students failed national exams, and in rural areas like Muhuru, nearly 80 percent of girls failed. When students failed to pass, they had no chance to progress on to tertiary education, rendering them stuck in their poor communities with limited economic opportunities. For all the immediate satisfaction Toni felt about her teacher incentive program, it had only helped a lucky subset of teachers and students.

What about everybody else? Was there a longer-term, more universal initiative that could be helpful to all Kenyan youth?

Although Toni's time in Muhuru was up in 2009 when she returned to education work in Harlem and applied to pursue an MBA, she did not jump ship on her Luo *dala*, her home. Staying in touch with the youth in the Luo community both online and on trips back to Muhuru, she started to think harder about the resources that most citizens already did have access to, and she realized that the most common denominator was a simple cell phone. Seeds of a solution emerged from her conversations with students: what if there existed a mobile phone application that assisted rural students with national exam preparation? Could something as simple as a set of educational text messages and phone-based games provide enough support to coach a student through the intimidating national evaluations?

With a deep-seated belief in the promise of the mobile app idea, and a remarkable leap of faith, Toni dropped out of business school, moved back to Kenya, and cofounded Eneza Education, a tech start-up that uses mobile phone technologies to share exam prep materials with students and help schools collect and analyze student performance data. Though based in Nairobi, often dubbed Africa's Silicon Valley, Toni still made the nine-hour drive out to Muhuru when she could, rumbling over cracked pavement and rocky earth, and riding cliffs that overlook the cradle of humankind's stunning, vast valley. In these moments, she found in herself a devotion to the Muhuru community—and a calm willingness to work on this education issue no matter how long it would take to see results.

But she found that most of her peers in Nairobi who also worked at the intersection of technology and social impact didn't have the same community roots, or the same patience for results. "In Nairobi you see an influx of social entrepreneurs, people who want to be hands-on with development," she said. "Many people end up pushing solutions on places where they simply don't have enough experience yet. So although they have good ideas, they have no idea if those ideas are welcome, or helpful. Most people are more interested in getting *something* done quickly than getting the *right thing* done."

Though Toni was pleased to be surrounded by socially conscious peers, she also lamented the influx of social entrepreneurs who expected to change the world simply with a few months of hard work. Many of her peers did not take Toni's approach to change: developing innovative ideas slowly over time and building deep roots in communities like Muhuru Bay, where she aspired to make a difference. Yet Toni can't imagine having succeeded any other way.

Toni's choice to remain patient with the pace of change in Muhuru has yielded incredible results so far. By designing a product with significant input from the rural students, Eneza Education's test prep app has spread virally to hundreds of thousands of student users at over one thousand schools across Kenya, growing at a rate of about one thousand users per day. In 2013, her team conducted a study that found that with two hours of mobile app use per week, students' average scores increased by thirty-seven points, compared to peers at the same schools with the same teachers, and that Eneza users held higher marks in every subject, especially in mathematics.

As Toni and her team grows Eneza Education's impact, she continues to become a more recognized leader in the fast-paced world of technology development. She keeps close to heart her self-awareness around the Western tendency to push for fast results, constantly checking it against her vibrant relationships with the Muhuru Bay community, which has proven to her that being patient and being highly effective with social change go hand-in-hand.

Everyday Ways to Be Patient

Toni's experience in understanding that change takes time rings true at every level of social change, even in our own neighborhoods. If you've ever volunteered at a soup kitchen or homeless shelter, you'll know that people accessing services are often there as a last resort while battling the stress of poverty. An impatience-prone volunteer engaging only in a one-off, token visit might feel like he or she is contributing very little toward authentically helping someone. But if the volunteer focuses instead on seeing the people they're serving simply as fellow people, not just as beneficiaries of goodwill, the volunteer receives an opportunity to form lasting relationships, connections that can transform perspective in positive ways.

This patient, relationship-based approach to social change can be fulfilled every time you participate in your local community, whether it's a one-off event or many events over time. Giving your time is just like giving your money, and even more valuable sometimes, and by placing more value on time as currency, you may find it easier to adopt an attitude of patience in your everyday interactions. Ever heard the phrase "throwing money at the problem"? It's not always a good thing. Sometimes, the desire to solve a problem quickly is admirable in the face of human suffering. However, the obstacle remains that lasting solutions rarely emerge from reactionary investments. Minimizing poverty, disease, or hunger requires financial investment but, more important, requires well-planned expenditures in the development of the people battling those challenges everyday. And those investments in people can take years to show returns. They don't emerge immediately, but they're worth waiting for.

For many everyday ambassadors, giving time is far more feasible than giving donations. The big problem that we need to overcome is the negative thinking that time isn't as meaningful a gift as money. A hierarchy of compassion emerges when the media singles out the lucky few who have the resources and opportunities to make immediate and big gifts; society ends up overlooking, or even devaluing, the many people who give their time, consistently and compassionately, without expectations of immediate results. These everyday ambassadors—teachers, mentors, religious leaders, parents, healthcare pro-

PATIENCE IN ACTION

Prentice Onayemi grappled with cultivating patience when he began conducting drama therapy sessions with survivors of the Liberian Civil War at the Buduburam Refugee Camp. "I definitely have wished many times that I could invest more time traveling to and working at the camp," he says. "But it's important to be honest with yourself about what you're able to give, especially when you are making promises with the people you are aiming to serve," Prentice says. "Ask yourself, 'What am I doing with my time?' Be as specific as possible when you answer."

viders, small-business owners, law enforcement officials, sanitation workers—make our cities and towns livable, clean, strong, and safe. When we start valuing our time as equal to money, we might find a stronger appreciation for making a difference over a longer period instead of expecting to see results quickly.

One interesting example of fostering the time-as-money ethos is a concept called TimeBanking, which originated in the 1990s and still thrives in many communities all over the world, from Los Angeles, California, to Otaki, New Zealand, to Brattleboro, Vermont. TimeBanking treats time very literally as money; members log on to post offers of services or skills to others, as well as requests for any help they need. Every hour you log helping someone earns you a TimeBank Hour, which you can then use to request time from others. All of the requests for time add up to more than each project; the consistent time spent with neighbors, in helpful ways, serves to strengthen a community by strengthening the bonds between its residents. Plenty of communities don't even need the formality of a TimeBank to play out these social norms; they simple expect that residents will band together to help others in times of need and receive help when they experience struggle. But the key, underpinning value to ensuring this type of a system functions properly is that of patience. Patience means giving our time abundantly and paying it forward, even if the reward takes a long time to emerge. Patience means seeing time and relationships as currency, treasures that lead to ultimately happier and healthier communities. As TimeBank describes its core belief, "Community is built upon sinking roots, building trust, creating networks."

How Patience Makes the Difference

It is of course understandable why this mindset isn't always simple to apply in our everyday lives, especially if we live in or make visits to communities where there is evident suffering and need for change. We often want to be helpful *now*! We want to see relief *now*! When feelings like this arise, I think of the story of Laura McNulty, an American woman who used to volunteer in the Dominican Republic on one-week medical service trips. Like most of us, Laura felt compelled to bring help to the impoverished, rural countryside she visited, and in her role as a temporary volunteer, she saw her chance to contribute.

But then, one day, things changed drastically. Laura stopped in to a poor household that was visited often by foreign medical missionaries (not just Laura's crew), and what she saw was shocking. "I'll never forget when we stepped into the patient's windowless, cement barrack home that day, and she pulled out three plastic baggies full of pills, of all shapes and sizes, no particular rhyme or reason." The medical mission that had visited the woman just weeks prior likely thought they were doing a service by providing her with medications she perhaps would have otherwise been unable to afford or too far from a pharmacy to purchase. But in this case, the pills signaled bad news to Laura. "Not one of the bags or the pills was labeled," she lamented. "Not even with the patient's name."

The patient had no idea what the pills were meant to manage. Although Laura was not a doctor, she could diagnose the situation for what it was: the herds of well-intentioned medical volunteers who had come through the village on short-term trips were clearly doing more harm than good. The lack of instructions or follow-up care from those missionaries meant the pills provided the woman more risk than relief. The drop-in doctors, despite their goodwill, provided that woman a low standard of healthcare.

Laura began reflecting on her own role as a short-term volunteer. "I was struck by the lack of continuity in my work. Nothing we did in the course of a one-week trip addressed underlying issues like insufficient access to high-quality healthcare and adequate sanitation, water, and nutrition." The brief medical service trips that defined much of Laura's college career began to feel futile. "We were holding medical consultations in makeshift clinics with no system of follow-up, no standardized medication formulary, no medical records. We had such minimal contact with the existing healthcare system that in many places we did not know there was an existing healthcare system," she said of the behaviors that made her feel uncomfortable. "People in the communities we served deserved the same level of quality care I would expect in the States. I knew there had to be a better way."

Rather than continue with the status quo, Laura instead dove headfirst into a more patient solution. With a former classmate, she moved full-time to the Dominican Republic in 2009 to found Health Horizons International (HHI), an organization that gives high-quality healthcare to even the poorest families in the country. Laura started without any expectation of quick results. She knocked on the door of every clinic, hospital, NGO, and poor household she could find to map the resources already in place, including their strengths and weaknesses, and to find out how she could fill critical gaps in care. "Finally we could do what we never were able to do on one-week trips: simply get to know people and listen to their experiences, worries, and dreams."

Laura fondly recalled sharing a meal of rice and beans and *jugo de chinola* with a local woman, bachata music blaring as the background to their animated discussions on the differences between perspectives on healthcare of the residents of the Dominican Republic and their neighbors in Haiti. "We covered so much ground in those personal moments, from the complications of structural racism, to language barriers, to cultural beliefs about healing," Laura said. She learned about environmental and socioeconomic factors that increased a patient's likelihood to contract infectious and chronic diseases and saw that local health systems were not resourced well enough to provide reliable care, meaning patients endured significant gaps in the continuity and quality of services they received. At the same time, Laura uncovered that dozens of women in the communities had already completed training programs in nursing techniques, vaccination, and first aid but were not working as health workers due to a lack of consistent resources and support at an organizational level.

From such patient conversations, Laura decided to use HHI to develop a cadre of *cooperadores de salud*, or community health workers. By hiring local women with existing healthcare skills—people with a constant presence in the community—HHI could help patients with chronic diseases, provide health education, and support public health projects in the community all at once. Hiring men and women who were raised in the communities they served gave HHI cultural intelligence to provide high-quality care and leadership. This avoided the risks of impatient, short-term volunteers who left existing local health systems in jeopardy.

"The local system is always weakened when people try to work around it instead of with it," Laura explained. "And then the cycle of illness continues." HHI still welcomes international volunteers, but they are assigned tasks within a framework that appropriately channels their dedication, energy, and expertise. By partnering with the cooperadores and local medical providers, these foreign volunteers engage in mutual learning and can serve their patients with the confidence that they will be cared for even after they leave. "My journey building HHI has taught me that when people are unwilling, or even unable, to commit to understanding the underlying drivers of surface problems, they often end up exacerbating the issue instead of becoming part of the solution," said Laura. "Short-term volunteers can inadvertently disempower local patients to participate in improving their own health." It's long-term vision and investment "that will change the game for good—for our patients, the local health system, and the communities we partner with."

Patience, as Laura's example demonstrates, is far more than the ability to wait for a web page to load without cursing. It is more than having the mental fortitude to not snap at a stranger in the face of uncontrollable delays. Patience is trusting that small acts of kindness with no immediate return will pay off in the end. Patience is believing that time investment in entire communities and healthy relationships is the cornerstone to effective service work.

Patience is relevant not only for people working formally in the social sector but for anyone aspiring to make a positive difference. At an everyday business level, customer service is founded on the philosophy of being patient with customers, yet this ethos is becoming ever harder to uphold in our digital world. Restaurant hosts and retailers, among many other business people, deal with digitally distracted customers on a daily basis: the people who complain when a meal or that cute dress in a different size isn't brought over immediately. What's worse is that customers' perceptions of immediacy are now even shorter than they used to be, as reported by Narayan Janakiraman at the University of Texas at Arlington in his 2011 study, "The Psychology of Decisions to Abandon Waits for Service." According to Janakiraman, our "need for instant gratification is not new, but our expectation of 'instant' has become faster, and as a result, our patience is thinner."[4] That may seem like ominous news for business owners, but the bright side is that every day brings new opportunities to shift the status quo and demonstrate patience to your customers that, over time and with repetition, will reflect well on you.

Patience is a concept also crucial in our simple, everyday interactions with family, friends, and ourselves. When our online pace transfers into offline interactions, we miss important details in body language and conversation. Mom might have said, as you hurried to wrap up the phone call, that "it's OK to miss Grandma's birthday party next week." But if you had been listening to her, really listening instead of rushing, you might have heard her intonation of disappointment and realized how much it meant to her for you to go. Overlooking details out of impatience can mean failing to see that someone is ailing or upset or can mean being oblivious to cries for help in which your intervention could, literally, be lifesaving.

There is a now famous story by Kent Nerburn, who discovered the power of patience while working a late-night shift as a taxi driver in Minneapolis, Minnesota. When he received a call in the middle of the night, Kent imagined the caller would fit the bill of those who normally call in the wee hours before dawn: a pie-eyed partier, an arguing lover, a worker with an early morning shift. Instead, he drove up to a quiet apartment building with just a single light glowing. Many drivers would have honked twice, waited a moment, and then driven away in such a precarious situation—the eeriness of the mostly dark building at 2:30 AM was difficult to ignore. But Kent possessed compassion and felt drawn to approach the front door, to see if the passenger needed any help.

Kent's instincts were right on. A frail, elderly woman came to the door, quite slowly, donning a veiled pillbox hat, "like you might see in a costume shop or a Goodwill store or in a 1940s movie," Kent wrote in an essay on the experience. She asked him to carry her small suitcase out to the car for her and then give her a few moments of solitude in her apartment. "Then, if you could come back and help me? I'm not very strong."

Kent followed her every request, imagining he'd want his own mother treated with kindness if she ever needed the help. In between her profuse thanks to Kent, she directed him toward her destination address but asked him to drive along a meandering route. She was headed to a hospice, she explained. With no family left, and a doctor's word that she didn't have long left to live, the woman saw this drive as a final good-bye to her home city. Kent immediately shut off the meter and asked her where she wanted to go. He wrote of that night:

> For the next two hours we drove through the city. She showed me the building where she had once worked as an elevator operator. We drove through the neighborhood where she and her husband had lived when they had first been married. She had me pull up in front of a furniture warehouse that had once been a ballroom where she had gone dancing as a girl. Sometimes she would have me slow in front of a particular building or corner and would sit staring into the darkness, saying nothing.[5]

As dawn crept along the skyline, the woman finally noted her fatigue; it was time for her to go to the hospice. Upon arrival, the woman asked what she owed, and Kent insisted, "You owe me nothing." Kent instead felt compelled to hug her, to thank her for giving him such a meaningful experience.

"You gave an old woman a little moment of joy," she told him in response. "Thank you."

In many ways, Kent's superpower that evening was simply that he exhibited more patience than others might have. He waited for a slow, elderly woman at a spooky building at a late hour when others would have driven away. He cared enough to ask her where she was going, engaging her in conversation when others might have just tried to get from point A to point B as quickly as possible. Kent reflected, powerfully, "How many other moments like that had I missed or failed to grasp? We are so conditioned to think that our lives revolve around great moments. But great moments often catch us unawares."[6]

Our life's more powerful interactions are indeed often the most unexpected, but we can encourage them to happen more often by giving them the time to happen. We have to have the patience and the presence of mind to slow down and appreciate small, seemingly insignificant moments so that they can become the great ones. If we cannot stop rushing, it becomes impossible to see the fullness of another human being in front of us, one who might truly need a moment of human connection.

Beyond our outreach to other people, being impatient with ourselves can also cause us to miss opportunities for growth and meaning. For example, if you do poorly on a task at work or on an exam, despite having tried your best, a normal reaction might be to self-hate or criticize. But instead of losing your temper, try being patient: think about where you need to go from this point, and figure out your next steps with a long view of your future. Set goals for yourself—whether related to work, love, or a hobby—that are realistic. Try to step back and bring a gentler and more reasonable mindset to planning. Success often requires morphing pressure into patience. That transformation starts with you.

A Final Word on Patience

Patience is relevant to an everyday ambassador's life at every level, not only with yourself and your immediate loved ones but also with people in your community who might otherwise be strangers. Anyone who has volunteered at a local level to help improve the lives of others knows how important it is to keep patience in mind throughout the process of service. Service is rarely ever an act of instant gratification. Sure, building a home with Habitat for Humanity or painting an uplifting mural on a neighborhood wall yields a specific, material product that can be celebrated in a short time frame. But more often, we engage in long-term projects, like tutoring in a classroom or mentoring in after-school programs, in which we invest our time and effort and may not see results for weeks, months, or even years.

Sometimes those results are measurable—your student scores the A you've been coaching her toward, or your mentee aces the job interview you've been preparing him for—however, more often, results are intangible, such as a student's self-esteem or improved classroom and professional behavior. These are changes that might happen very slowly, and it can be a deeply frustrating experience if you expect a fast turnaround. Investing over time, even if it's only once a week or twice a month, demonstrates a consistency and devotion that is a necessary first step to developing any relationship and doing any socially impactful work.

The same goes for work at a broader, global level, where there is something not only necessary but also sacred about cultivating patience, especially in our fast-paced world. When confronted with the harsh problems of disease and poverty that exist in some of the poorest places on the planet, it can be easy to feel overwhelmed by the combination of guilt that we *must do something* and powerlessness that there's nothing one person can do to end a pandemic or reverse the cycle of poverty. This means we end up too paralyzed to do anything. Focusing on patience instead forces us to think, in a healthy way, about our own limitations: admitting that there are things we have yet to learn and valuing the time it takes to build relationships, forge friendships, and develop networks of partners that will enhance and expand our learning. As Toni, Laura, and Kent demonstrate, the power of their social impact was based heavily on their abilities to stick by a cause and by communities and people over time. They are examples of people who practice patience, whether through dedication to one cause or community over many years or with a single human being over a simple cab ride.

Patience, ultimately, is the acceptance of imperfection. Bus schedules and internet algorithms are, most of the time, reliably on point. Family relationships, significant others, and most plans for social change are notoriously imperfect. In our quest to improve a strained relationship or dire situation, patience is the irreplaceable daily practice that reminds us: high speed usually doesn't result in high impact.

Cultivating Patience

It's easy to become impatient these days. With so many components of our lives available at the touch of a button—purchasing and returning clothes, ordering food, depositing checks—it can seem like patience is a thing of the past, not even something we legitimately need anymore. But in reality, patience is crucially important in our households, in our work, and in other daily interactions, especially when connecting with others in a real and meaningful way—online, offline, and all the lines in between.

Patience protects us from the trap of becoming overwhelmed by the endless responsibilities we are faced with, whether they're related to a social cause or to our familial and friendship duties, and reminds us to take things one step at a time, one day at a time. Patience reminds us that more important than a quick, superficial "win" is the success brought by a long and hard-fought commitment to a cause or to another person.

As a quick reminder, the questions and exercises below have three distinct purposes: the inner reflections are for you to work through by yourself; the outer reflections are for you to do in a group or with at least one other person, to get an idea of what others are thinking and to help you become clearer about how you want to present your opinions to others; and the action steps are to help you translate all this thinking into real-life activity.

Inner Reflections

- How many news articles did I read in *full* today, compared with how many headlines I simply skimmed? What am I risking by skimming instead of reading? What norms am I developing?

- There are both benefits and dangers to having access to seemingly endless amounts of instant information online; sometimes the access empowers us to be better informed, other times it can feel overwhelming, and we end up in an information paralysis. Think of examples in the past week when you've felt empowered by, and overwhelmed by, the digital deluge of instantaneous info. When you feel overwhelmed, how do you respond?

- Sometimes, the sound-bite style communication of our online lives can trickle into our offline behavior. Think back to the most recent argument you had with someone. Did you ever find yourself exchanging quick quips instead of sitting down for an extended conversation? What are the pros and cons of both types of conflict resolution?

Outer Reflections

- If you haven't yet, come up with a sixty second elevator pitch about the type of service work you're involved in or interested in and try it on the group. What feels like it's missing, and how do you think we can learn to have deeper conversations in a world where fast-paced pitching is often a necessary norm?

- Have you ever felt pressured to show the results of your work even before there were results to show? How did you respond when someone else in your professional or personal life lacked patience? What are tips for others to handle this pressure gracefully?

- When problems arise, do you ever feel pressured to solve them quickly, even if they deserve much longer consideration? Which components of your work get put at risk if you rush to achieve results?

Action Steps

- Think about a cause you care for deeply or a problem you are intent on solving. Try to explain, in 140 characters or less, the root of the problem. Now try, again in 140 characters, to explain the best solution to the problem. What aspects of the problem and solution were you unable to discuss when faced with conditions of brevity? Make a plan that will convince your audiences to move from the brief pitch to a longer discussion.

- No matter how many different causes you are engaged with, focus on one and set a goal for yourself that will be achieved over the next twelve months. It could be giving a few more hours of your time every week to an organization, galvanizing a new number of supporters, or providing a specific type of service. Check back in with a group of similarly committed friends, and encourage one another to be patient and persistent.

- We're sometimes conditioned to expect, or at least yearn for, relatively instant feedback and recognition for our efforts. One way to combat this tendency is to see ourselves, not only as individual achievers, but as members of larger teams. Determine ways that you can begin sharing your spotlight and highlight the contributions of your full team and coworkers in order to actively fight the desire for immediate recognition.

PUTTING EVERYDAY AMBASSADORSHIP TO WORK

When there is no enemy within,
the enemies outside cannot hurt you.

—Unknown

Just one month before the 2012 United States presidential election, I had the opportunity to hear US Secretary of Defense Leon Panetta address a room of mostly millennial innovators, hailing from all over the globe and gathered at the Academy of Achievement's summit in Washington, DC. When asked to reflect on his definition of the world's severest security issue, Panetta didn't skip a beat before replying, "The greatest threat to the United States of America in the twenty-first century is not Al Qaeda. It is the inability for Americans, particularly our elected representatives, to find common ground."

Secretary Panetta's remark struck me as particularly powerful, as I was in the midst of penning *Everyday Ambassador*, aspiring to convince compassionate people of the need for connecting on a human level. I hadn't yet considered the disconnectivity paradox as a notable issue beyond the sphere of millennials and others engaged in social impact work. Yet here it was, emerging as an urgent concern affecting domestic affairs and international relations alike, a concern that our own polarization and disconnectivity at home was even more dangerous than the extension of enemies abroad. An issue I thought was originally relegated to Millenials' personal development was actually pressing enough to concern one of the world's most senior defense officials.

Notably, Secretary Panetta wasn't referencing the squabbles of twentysomethings not seeing eye-to-eye. His was a nod to the oft-childish arguments of his peers, the older, presumably wiser, and more socialized generations, whose disagreements and unforgiving partisanship put national welfare at risk. Beyond Secretary Panetta's point about our elected officials, there are other obvious ways that a lack of common ground threatens national security, namely in the form of extremists who engage in hate crimes and terrorism against citizens of other countries (and of their own countries). Tracing the roots of a homophobic aggressor, for example, often reveals that the attacker had no openly gay friends, had never been educated about sexual identity, and oftentimes personally had suffered from stifled sexual identity or sexual abuse. Similarly tragic is the ongoing violence against American Sikhs, whose head coverings signal to uneducated assailants that they are "Muslim terrorists." These attacks demonstrate gross misunderstandings on multiple levels: Sikhism is in no way related to Islam, which in turn is by no means an indicator of terrorist behavior. But because the attackers have consumed so much hateful propaganda and experienced such minimal interaction with people of either Muslim or Sikh faiths, their aggression persists, proving nothing but their own paranoia regarding terrorism.

These visibly destructive results of our disconnectivity are undoubtedly the most harrowing. Thankfully, because they are rooted in such intense emotion and deep misunderstanding, we can more easily identify them as examples of bad behavior. In response, we can quickly prescribe solutions like more education for our children about diversity, more tolerance to be taught in schools, or more campaigns to be created that honor the positive powerful nature of diverse societies. We can try to prevent future conflicts by targeting the source of the hatred: extremists often feel that they have nothing in common with their victims; it is the fear and misunderstanding of their victim that fuels extremists to stamp out what they perceive to be foreign and thus dangerous.

More difficult to pinpoint, and far more complicated to fix, are the disconnectivities that occur in the moments when we believe we are most connected. Too often we see examples like the group of volunteers in Indonesia, in which impatient individuals (even if well-intentioned) set out to change the world but end up pedaling backward. I realize that my own susceptibility to many of these attitudes increases as months and years pass, and my digital engagement becomes more closely integrated into my life. For example, whether I need an instant chat with Asfaw and my Ethiopian team while home in America or need to quickly contact my family while working from Addis, no matter if I'm on the go with my smartphone or sitting with my laptop, I can always get in touch immediately. But in spite of such brilliant convenience, I face the new challenge of cultivating patience in the face of major project delays. I know I should be patient, but I'm so accustomed to rapid resolutions that it remains a struggle to stay calm.

Similarly, I find myself many days numb to urgent requests from colleagues, so swallowed up in excessive emails and an inbox overflowing with deliverables from countless initiatives. Despite my self-awareness of the dangers of multitasking, I feel perpetually on the brink of being spread too thin, habituated to thumbing through my smartphone to shoot off quick replies in pockets of travel time (at the risk of running into fellow pedestrians on the sidewalk). I have to deliberately remind myself during one-on-one interactions to forget about my device and provide friends the undivided attention they deserve.

When we find ourselves too regularly in states of distraction and flurries of activity, our connections to others become increasingly superficial, oftentimes without our awareness. These numerous, subtle, yet sadly frequent failures at being kind, attentive, and mature, at interacting in focused, empathetic, humble, and patient ways, are hugely detrimental. While we may not even notice this behavior, the person on the other end of the exchange surely will. Even the best intentions will never translate into the change we hope to facilitate.

Considering the digital social environments pressuring us, we must begin to fight back. We must cultivate an internal counterforce that reminds us of focus, empathy, humility, and patience. We must step away from habits like scrolling through friends' Facebook profiles, Twitter feeds, and GIF-filled Tumblr sites with an underlying tone of one-upmanship, and instead use these tools actively, for the purpose of lasting human connection. We must use social media and online tools for truly corrective purposes to learn a new language, develop a shareable skill, or exchange ideas with someone we would otherwise never meet. We must pursue a state of online consciousness and avoid the tendency to open new browser tabs in order to escape, to avoid opportunities for enhancing our offline lives—our *real* lives.

Being online conscious will only become a *more* important skill as digital connectivity becomes more closely intertwined with our lives and more fundamental to our every interaction. The more our devices and digital platforms become part of our identities, the more we must remind ourselves that we are human apart from them. We can choose to embrace the positive angles of connection—like staying in touch for free with friends from different continents or seeing photos of a new baby cousin from halfway across the country—and we can choose to discard the negatives. Social comparisons do nothing but provoke inner insecurities.

A habit of conscious appreciation for the wonders of instant communication will then translate smoothly into a life of everyday ambassadorship. The goal of being a good global citizen hints at the importance of acknowledging our planet's new digital interconnectedness, and many everyday ambassadors travel the world to build relationships and cross borders at the international level. But the term *global citizen* too readily evokes requirements of having a flight itinerary or passport in hand. Unlike the global citizen in image, but similar in spirit, the everyday ambassador may never leave her hometown but realizes that the way she interacts with the world, on an everyday basis, in person and in online spaces, can make international ripples, for better or for worse. An everyday ambassador may not rack up many passport stamps, but he makes wise decisions about the causes he supports, the products he buys, and the language he uses to interact with others. An everyday ambassador takes advantage of the abundant opportunities that now exist to make *and* maintain far-off relationships that add vibrant details to his understanding of the world, of his own country and culture, and he uses that knowledge and understanding to build bridges back to his own home communities, linking people who may not otherwise have the opportunity to interact. Being an everyday ambassador means respecting differences and striving to find common ground, whether with a person from another nation or religion or with a next-door neighbor or family member.

With the continued proliferation of digital connectivity comes an increasing number of opportunities to connect with and remain linked to people you would otherwise never meet. But how can you be sure that you're approaching these relationships in an ambassadorial way, in a manner that allows you to have not only the greatest possible immediate social impact but also the most lasting human connection as well? No matter your location, circumstance, or passions, the lessons of the everyday ambassador offer a powerful exercise in self-reflection—and that inner change is a skill that's impossible to download or copy and paste into your life. But keeping in your heart the four key principles—and the following nine suggestions—make everyday ambassadorship a lifestyle that is entirely within your grasp.

1. **Grow closer to faraway people—but not further away from people close by.** If *Everyday Ambassador* had a golden rule, this would be it. In an increasingly digital world, it's crucial to note that technology is not the problem. The problem is how we choose to use the tools at our disposal. If we want to be the most connected we can be to other people, whether it's through online or offline mechanisms, the single rule we need to keep in mind is one of proximity. On the one hand, we can make incredible efforts via technology to grow closer to people we live far away from. Until teleportation is invented, there will always be prohibitively high costs to traveling to see someone in person, and so we need to employ Skype, FaceTime, text messaging, phone calls, and every social media platform available to be in touch. However, it's not just good enough to use those platforms—we need to use them thoughtfully. It's easy to have Skype running but really still be looking at other things online or checking the phone for messages. It's even easier to multitask when no video is involved, and be in a text conversation with someone while you're en route to work or at the office, where an interruption could easily cause you to pause, confusing the other person. If you're going to connect with someone who is far away and try to make that person feel close to you, then you need to use technology in ways that mimic your really being there with that person, and you need to give your undivided attention.

   On the other hand, we have to be just as careful to not let technology pull us further from people already close by. That starts with the basics: keep your phone tucked away when you talk to other people directly, make meal times device-free times at home and in the workplace, and consider actually talking to someone on your daily commute instead of getting caught up in Candy Crush. But it goes beyond these basics as well. There are now so many ways that our distracted digital behaviors trickle into our offline lives that even in circumstances where we're unplugged and device free, we might not be present or considerate in our conversations. Our minds may have become so wired to wander that we can't hear between the lines of what someone is trying to say to us. Maybe a friend is relating a story to you in which she is trying to reveal a difficult piece of information, waiting for you to pick up on her cues and ask more to let her unload her burden. The more deeply engaged you become in conversations, the more you'll be able to truly connect.

2. **Understand broadly but commit deeply.** The first tech trap we discussed is one that interrupts our ability to stay focused on a person or a cause when the going gets tough—anything that minimizes our courage to keep fighting for what we believe in or pushes us to be distracted from our goal. Focus is understandably a difficult thing to foster in a world where we regularly communicate in 140 characters; ours is a sound-bite culture where our relevance can only survive by the wits of our memes and the quips in our comments—not through in-depth analysis. And in a world of constant refreshing of screens and feeds offering updated links and articles, in the face of constant distractions pulling us in multiple directions, it can feel impossible to focus on a single issue or item. If we're not careful, this can quickly translate to an attitude that lends to habits of concession and surrender—and ultimately, unwillingness and indifference.

   Commitment to one place or cause is clearly a challenge for people who choose to travel frequently. But it's also a challenge for those of us who live in a very consistent, defined community. Taking everyday opportunities to change our norms can thus be therapeutic and self-strengthening. Think about, for instance, anytime you flip open your laptop or log on online. How many browser windows end up being open at any given time? How many substantive articles do you actually *read*, and how many do you never quite get through? How many unread documents are sitting in your downloads folder? How many unfinished files are on your desktop or saved to your hard drive? Part of living in a digital world is the immense blessing of having seemingly (or actually) limitless hard drive space and cloud storage to store our many ideas and interests, but consciously organizing ourselves (and scaling down, with the necessities—not the excesses—in mind) to follow through is a difficult yet ultimately empowering practice.

Every time we say no to something we don't believe we can really commit to, it enables us to say yes to something to which we truly intend to stay devoted. The more we can cultivate these practices in our digital lives, the more they will trickle into our interactions with people offline. In the home environment, this can have the immense benefit of making us more present and available for friends, family members, and neighbors. Others will trust us to be involved in their lives when it is believable that we're willing to put away our devices and focus on their needs. In the greater world of social impact, whether we choose to volunteer or work at home or abroad, being more focused leads us, inevitably, to being more effective with the issue we feel drawn to support. We have to repeat to ourselves as a mantra that it's not our individual job to save the world, end AIDS, or bring education to every child. But it might be our job, and can be our chosen focus, to make sure no one in our town goes hungry, or give all teenagers in one high school free access to confidential HIV testing, or ensure that all students in one neighborhood have support to report bullies. Take the big issues that motivate your social conscious and break them up into doable pieces. Then take a laser-like focus to making sure that each specific piece gets done.

3. **Enjoy your digital bubble but burst it every so often.** The key here is thinking about consciousness in our everyday actions, the type of thoughtfulness that signals to another person, *Even if I don't have your life experience, I'd like to understand it.* Having empathy is a step beyond being able to focus; it implies not only that you're present and giving undivided attention but also that you're actively making an effort to understand something that you otherwise would have no knowledge of.

   Unfortunately, this is a difficult value to emulate when we're stripped of the need for consciousness in our everyday online lives. Remember that your search engine feeds you information linked to what you have sought out before, posts ads that cater to your preexisting interests, and reminds you most prominently of the sites that you frequent. If you want to expand past your own digital bubble and actually be exposed to ideas and people who challenge your beliefs and realities, you'll need to make a conscious effort to do so.

   For example, think about whom you follow on Twitter and who shows up on your feed. For most people, such a tool is used to stay updated about friends and about issues, organizations, and news they have a passion for. But are there other ways that Twitter could be used to build more empathy? What if you tried following a politician from a different party, a leader from a religious group that is different from yours, or someone interested in your industry but from a different country? The pure exposure to viewpoints we may disagree with is a healthy exercise that prevents us from becoming stagnant thinkers, boxed into a specific set of talking points, yet it is one that barely anyone encounters in a highly customizable digital world. Who knows? You might even end up finding that you appreciate or have something in common with someone you thought was completely different from you.

This becomes a priceless exercise once the benefits of developing empathy sweep into our lives off of social media sites. Knowing more about the full scope of views on a particular issue means we can speak with more grace and care in group environments and be less likely to accidentally insult or ostracize another person whose perspective we otherwise wouldn't know existed. We can be more aware of cultural and generational sensitivities, and we can sharpen our own arguments about issues so that we avoid careless insults and instead craft more meaningful and compelling talking points that might encourage others to follow our social missions.

For example, my Facebook feed is the kind that is mostly filled with liberal sentiments, including bold language and links to harsh commentary on gun control and why America needs to rein in gun ownership in order to save lives. It's a position I've always affiliated with, but without realizing it, I also accepted the mischaracterization of gun owners as backward, uneducated, citizens who are knowingly promoting innocent deaths by insisting on their right to carry a firearm. When I finally had an opportunity to debate the topic with a group of public service peers online, I was surprised to hear viewpoints from many progun advocates. They explained from their side the concerns about how much the government should control a person's private life and made accurate points as to how few and far between gun deaths were in their more remote parts of the country. Their perspectives didn't change my deep beliefs about gun control, but they certainly were enough to make me realize that I had been demonizing a group of people I didn't even understand. Appreciating the diversity of viewpoints within my community of public service devotees taught me to bring more nuance into my arguments, and see people as more than the stereotype of apolitical viewpoint.

4. **It's all about you, but don't let it be.** The third trap that technology can lead us into is marked by entitlement and distorted self-importance—that which reduces our capacity for humility. On a daily if not minute-by-minute basis, we live in a world of expected status updates, i-everything accounts, and .me domain names. Rarely are we rewarded for acknowledging our weaknesses, and the limitless availability of information at our fingertips has made it less acceptable than ever before to not know something. As a result, we develop not only an inner defensiveness but, if we're not careful, a misleading guise of external expertise as well—one that needlessly intimidates and alienates.

   Many of us may not have the chance to learn these lessons in some globe-trotting, service-focused way, but everyday opportunities to test and strengthen our capacities for humility abound. One primary place is in our posts to Facebook, Twitter, Instagram, or any social media site. We may act in self-centered ways or use our profiles as a way to create a limiting image of ourselves. Think about all the ways you share with the digital world and consider setting up a few rules for yourself, at the least a conscious set of questions by which you decide whether or not (and what) to share. It could be worth asking each time you do share something, *Am I posting this just to craft my reputation, or is it actually something important for others to know?* Try to create quotas for yourself and make a majority (or at least half) of your posts dedicated to shouting out the good work or wise words of someone whom you admire or want to show appreciation for, or posting content that you think someone else would find interesting or helpful and tagging that person. These are powerful ways to use the everyday Facebook platform that diminish our inflated self-importance and still allow us to be active members of social networks.

Offline, a practice could be consciously telling someone when you don't know the answer instead of going immediately to an internet search. There's no shame in not knowing, and this is especially the case if you're trying to learn. When you raise your hand to ask a clarifying question in class or at a work meeting, this is not only good for you and the nurturing of your humility, but also it is good for your fellow classmates and coworkers, for whom you are breaking social-norm barriers and signaling that it is safe and acceptable to still have something to learn, to value others' opinions, and to stay eternally teachable.

5. **Demand change but set reasonable expectations.** The last tech trap mentioned was the tendency to be impatient, a natural result of being ensconced in a world of immediate updates and instantly available information. When it's so much more efficient and oftentimes more comfortably nonconfrontational to search online for an answer rather than ask another human being for help, we gradually minimize such exchanges in our lives, a habit that can become detrimental if we start becoming impatient with interactions that rightfully require time and a slow pace. Most relationships, whether friendly, romantic, familial, or collegial, cannot be managed well if we're always expecting others to move at our pace and don't have the patience to allow for the time required to resolve differences and conflicts.

Interactions that require time and patience—like correspondence, shared meals, and hobbies—are not any less accessible than they were in a predigital world, but they're certainly things we must make time for nowadays and not expect will come our way naturally. Start with something simple, like writing a letter and mailing it, instead of writing an email, if it's about something you don't need an urgent answer on. Pay attention to the way you write when you put a pen to paper versus when you let your fingers fly across the keyboard. Are there words that come to you in a more patient medium that might escape you when it only takes seconds to type them up, and when they can be rewritten, deleted, or shared instantly and easily? Another example is sitting and eating a meal with others instead of grabbing takeout or making an instant meal, or taking up a hobby like gardening, which requires patience over time to see results. Deliberately engage in activities that actively help you develop a keener patience for change and growth.

Don't let yourself be lulled into thinking that slower, more careful movement and waiting on others (who will depend on your care over a period of time) are bothersome practices or not worthwhile. These are precious moments, and you must create these opportunities in your life to practice patience; otherwise, it won't come easily when you need it the most.

6. **Go abroad, with the right guide.** You might already be someone who travels frequently, or perhaps the stories in this book have inspired you to go abroad. If you're planning to engage in service work outside of a solo trip, then it is absolutely necessary to link up with a legitimate organization. There are many well-intentioned (as well as not well-intentioned) service organizations in the world that actually do far more bad than good to the communities they aim to serve.

To be aware of what makes an organization legitimate, consider some of the gold-standard organizations, like the Foundation for Sustainable Development (FSD) led by Mireille Cronin Mather. FSD engages participants in service projects that contribute toward long-term investments in communities and not short-run excursions that only benefit a volunteer's resumé. As Mireille has described, "FSD positions a participant as a facilitator and not as a doer. We take them out of their comfort zone of 'doing all the time' and ask them instead to listen, observe, learn, and build relationships. Nothing that can quite be checked off of a list." FSD's philosophy is framed as one of "honoring the human relationship" between a foreign volunteer and the community with whom they will be living. "We try to omit from our approach to development the idea that 'foreign is better,'" Mireille said. "Our partner communities have the capacity to make change for themselves and we ask students to help reveal those capacities."

Another excellent example is Global Citizen Year (GCY), whose founder and director, Abby Falik, is a pioneer at the forefront of a new movement encouraging American high school graduates to take "bridge years"—formal delays in the transition to college for the purpose of traveling the world and, in the cases of those involved with GCY, going on service missions. GCY's eight-month program gives volunteers something they don't always get in short-term programs: time. GCY expects its participants to learn the language of their destination, at least conversationally, and gives volunteers time to "sit through layers of preconception and peel back layers of the onion," said Abby. "By the time they come back, most say they 'didn't do anything' in their first four months, besides forming a number of relationships." But this period of relationship formation—no results, no fast action—has a "profound impact" on the participants, according to Abby. She believes that by the time volunteers reach eight months in-country, they may only *begin* to feel they are hitting their stride, an important note on just how long it can take to deeply learn about a community.

Finally, consider the work of Thinking Beyond Borders (TBB). Cofounded and directed by Robin Pendoley, TBB provides young people with gap-year opportunities that engage them in solving global issues, including health, education, environmental, and economic issues. Unlike many peer nonprofit and nongovernmental organizations, TBB creates partnerships with local organizations in the communities being served, agencies eager to share their expertise with students who are passionate about finding solutions. "We are aware that while volunteers' intentions are good, international volunteering as part of tourism—*voluntourism*—often causes far more harm than good," Robin has said.

According to Robin, there are two considerations we must make before we can have a meaningful, socially responsible cultural exchange. First, we must be ready to "identify our skill sets, a humbling exercise at any age, including an assessment of our limitations. Without knowledge of local customs and social systems, we cannot tailor our work to ensure it aligns with the existing culture of the community; this is a process that can legitimately take years." Second, we must consider that "what one perceives as a need in someone else's community may not actually be needed or even wanted."

In a majority of cultures around the world, turning away a gift like volunteer help when it is offered is rude, even if it is something that the community doesn't want to accept. While we want to do something for the community, we end up doing something *to* the community. And it may not be a good—or appreciated—thing. As an organization built on the principle of humility, TBB sends its volunteers out into the world with an important belief: that no matter how poor or needy a person may seem, that person has valuable knowledge and wisdom to share as well. "When we recognize this, we are on our way to being able to doing something *with* other communities rather than to them," Robin said.

7. **Stay at home and step outside your comfort zone.** Many of the everyday ambassadors featured in this volume are involved in work far beyond their homelands, across oceans and continents. But ambassadorship doesn't require a passport. Most nations are continuously becoming more diverse with the increased ease of global migration, and our differences extend well beyond ethnicity. Within even our own cities and neighborhoods, we can easily cross racial, religious, economic, and cultural borders.

   Think about the city or town that you call home. Think about how frequently you interact with people you meet—people who are different from you. If it's a low ratio, then aren't there plenty of borders for you to cross already? The opportunities abound; they could be at entertainment events, cultural festivals, church services, or at clubs and groups that can introduce you to something completely new, albeit right around the corner from the place you call home. There is also a complementary exercise that involves inviting people along whom you otherwise may have never thought to include into your world. Even if you're convinced someone won't take you up on the offer, provide opportunities anyway to bring together different friend, peer, or interest groups and discover ways in which you can be a bridge among people. It doesn't require any type of extroversion to be a connector in this capacity—just a willingness to facilitate cross-cultural exchanges.

These kinds of small, everyday outreach actions are crucial ways to foster a cultural revolution in which individuals embrace diversity instead of fear it; they allow us to more confidently venture across unfamiliar borders within our own communities, which may be a matter of stretching across the aisle. It is, after all, the discrimination of people who differ from us, be it conscious or subconscious, that exacerbates the spread of misunderstanding; it's the us-versus-them mentality that justifies inexcusable opportunity gaps. When you look at someone who has full-sleeve tattoos, someone who wears a cross, someone who wears a hijab, someone in baggy pants and a hoodie, someone wearing skinny jeans and Warby Parkers, or someone wearing a polo shirt with a popped collar, what goes through your mind? Be acutely aware of the ways in which you stereotype someone before you know anything about that person.

Crossing our comfort zones rarely requires an international flight, and it must occur on some level if we want to access the shared humanity that seems to be slipping away in a world of technological self-sufficiency.

8. **When it comes to your wallet, invest wisely.** Let's say that you aren't able to travel internationally, and it's just as unlikely that you'll be crossing any intimidating borders in your own home environment, as you're not quite ready to make such a leap yet. There are still important considerations to make in your everyday transactions; even your investments speak to what kind of an everyday ambassador you are.

For sure, we've all been bombarded with a plethora of new purchasing options in terms of setting the world right. In the supermarket, we can choose food that is fair trade, ensuring that we only buy from companies who treat people well throughout the entire supply chain. The same can be said now for many jewelry and retail products, where artisans in far-off countries are making fair living wages, and all we have to do is pay a slightly higher margin for the goods. This is positive change.

There are, however, also a set of misleading options on the store shelves, and these most often come in the form of buy-one-give-one models whereby purchasing a product means another one of those products will be donated to a person in need in a poor country. A popular example of this is the shoe company TOMS, which promises to give a free pair of shoes to a child in need overseas when you buy TOMS footwear. While there is immense nobility in such an initiative, there is also a risk of doing harm to the communities being served if giving away free products within a market financially harms the local people who otherwise would sell that product. Local entrepreneurs (who have their own families to care for) will lose business, whether it's shoes, T-shirts, or books being donated. Also, it is unsettling that buy-one-give-one business models rely on the *continuation* of poverty in order to stay profitable. Companies like TOMS have been quickly responsive to critiques from concerned customers who didn't support the business's overarching model. New approaches which keep the welfare of the target community at heart include manufacturing shoes, and thus creating new jobs, in the communities where shoes are donated.

Although often problematic, charity products are not always unwelcome, nor should we stifle our compassionate instincts. But a certain set of questions can help you avoid getting caught up in the mess. First, put yourself in the place of the person you *think* your purchase is helping and imagine if someone were making the same donation to your community; are there any potentially negative ways in which someone else's goodwill could do damage? Second, after you use a tool like Charity Navigator to check in on an organization's reputation, always conduct your own research—ask not just what the company self-promotes in marketing campaigns but what the *beneficiaries* actually have to say about it independently. If this type of information isn't available, then perhaps question your purchase.

Being an everyday ambassador in a fully globalized economy means being an active, informed, responsible consumer. If you love a style of shoes and want them even though you feel uncomfortable about the brand, you can still choose to go ahead and purchase them, but write a letter or an email or a Facebook post to the company so it knows your concerns. Only if enough customers become well-informed about dangerous donation or manufacturing models and report their dissatisfaction to the company will things change.

9. **Serve others, but only if it serves you too.** Here's the most important thing. The reason most people don't consider themselves everyday ambassadors or someone who changes the world is because they believe the passion, interest, or industry that they love just isn't a good fit for doing good. But in reality, people who work outside traditional service areas of health, education, and social services are perhaps the most important everyday ambassadors on the planet.

   Are you a computer science professional or student? Check out the Digital Humanitarian Network, which links professional humanitarian organizations with volunteer, technically skilled professionals during major disasters to find ways to customize existing technologies for social good. Maybe you're into design and construction, in which case organizations all over the world, like Engineers Without Borders and Architects Without

Borders, could use your help to build smarter clinics, schools, and social service infrastructures. If you love production and filmmaking, look into the work of Jubilee Project on YouTube and consider how you also can make meaningful films for social change. Opportunities abound for professionals in the performing arts to put their skills to good use, whether it's by offering training and tutoring to low-income or underprivileged youth in your community or serving with nonprofit organizations like Artists Striving to End Poverty, which connects talented artists with underserved youth around the world to help them become more empowered and eventually break the cycles of poverty in which they have been born.

You can also shoot for the stars and strive to become the next Tupac, TLC, or Alicia Keys, artists whose music carries powerful social change messages across radio waves and into listeners' hearts. If you're into fashion, get involved with groups like Indego Africa, a social enterprise that empowers female artisans in Rwanda by selling their unique handicrafts in collaboration with high-end designers and brands. Or if you are instead in the field of law and legal aid, opportunities are abundant, whether you work as a public interest lawyer or you take on pro bono cases to provide legal aid to people who would otherwise have no access. Heck, even if you just like to bake in your pajamas in your own kitchen, you can try Cissé Trading Co. cocoa baking mixes and be a part of this company's manufacturing of fair trade, non-GMO, and fully traceable sweets.

Another exciting field for making a difference is social entrepreneurship, in which a business approach is applied to social change initiatives. This trend is taking flight in western nations as well as locales all over the planet, and not only through foreigners attempting to disrupt traditional, top-down models of foreign aid. Even in the world's economically poorest countries, innovative minds are inventing and engineering fresh ideas that, at a community level, bring prosperity without the need for foreign saviors—check out the work of Global Minimum in Sierra Leone or the Akirachix in Kenya for inspiration. These organizations give young people opportunities to learn and practice engineering and software coding in order to create solutions for their communities.

All this considered, it will soon no longer be the norm for only select sectors to be considered worthy of doing service. Sure, we'll continue to need phenomenal teachers, physicians, counselors, and social workers. But beyond these established norms, *every* sector has the potential to do good in the world. So take your unique passion seriously!

Truly, the opportunities to make a positive difference in the world are as endless as you can imagine them to be. The key is to rethink service not as giving something to someone in need but as engaging in a two-way exchange, so both parties are motivated to offer something of importance. It's actually incredibly important that we choose careers and activities for ourselves that are well attuned to our skills and talents; if we don't love what we're doing, how can we consider our actions a gift of service to someone else? The world is always better off when we find ways to weave our respective talents into larger efforts.

Whatever it is that you, uniquely, have to offer, the world is waiting for you.

GRASSROOTS DIPLOMACY, GLOBAL IMPACT

> Thus travel spins us round in two ways at once: It shows us the sights and values and issues that we might ordinarily ignore; but it also, and more deeply, shows us all the parts of ourselves that might otherwise grow rusty.
>
> —Pico Iyer

Years ago, I experienced a crystal clear awakening when a group of well-intentioned but shortsighted international volunteers descended upon my Indonesian office with hearts of gold but an unintelligible game plan. It was a pivotal moment that sparked my passion for promoting good global citizenship—or what I now call everyday ambassadorship—setting me off on a journey to identify and learn from people like the ambassadors featured in this book. Yet such a moment of enlightenment did not come solely from the contrast between these volunteers' poor assumptions and the ambassadorial approach I believe is best practice. My frustration at their approach was in many ways a reflection of my *own* misdirected diplomacy on voyages past and my subsequent desire to make sure others would avoid similar follies.

I can still remember it as if it were yesterday: graduating high school and leaving my homogenous, tight-knit hometown for the vast, deserted plains of rural Mexico on a mission to build a home for a homeless family. Sparkling intentions in tow, intent on leaving the place better than I had found it, I recall feeling physically sickened within days of arriving, deeply disturbed by the poverty around me, unable to believe it was someone's actual reality. The mother who would inhabit the new home was exactly my age (seventeen), but she, with her three children huddled around her calves, had no high school education. She wept with gratitude for the four walls and roof we erected, despite the lack of electricity or plumbing. She now had shelter, but she would still need to walk a mile to use the bathroom—a filthy, ramshackle latrine propped up in an otherwise empty savanna, housing a toilet filled to the brim with stinking human waste.

How much of a favor was I really doing her family?

I felt crippled by my complete inability to do anything meaningful in the life of this seventeen-year-old mother. Considering her homelessness, lack of education, extreme poverty, and poor health, I felt powerless in the face of such a struggle. In my increasingly digital social interactions, I was an expert at doing—I could multitask across platforms and applications, and even while still in high school, I had a penchant for taking on many responsibilities at once. But in this case, I felt unable to focus on anything. The sheer weight of her suffering sat heavy in my heart, and I couldn't think of a single way to help her tackle the monstrous issues she faced.

During our downtime throughout the project, I challenged myself to modify that mindset, to think less about the overwhelming obstacles this woman faced and more about the small things I could do, such as, what we were there to do, building her a home. Beyond our concrete end product, I also thought harder about the abstract process of building a relationship with someone so different from me. Didn't that matter as well? Giving her undistracted time to share more about her life, and ask me about mine, I created the foundation on which we could both feel better off for having met and interacted. I tapped into a focus I hadn't employed in a long time—breaking down the big picture into manageable pieces—and I clung to it as I crossed the border back into the United States.

Almost one year later, I signed up for a spring break service trip to Guatemala City, trying to ignore the majority of my fellow college freshman posting to Facebook plans of beach vacations or nightclub parties. I wanted a second chance to approach a volunteer gig in a more focused, prepared way, and so I tried to do far more research about Guatemala *before* arriving at the urban orphanage, the *hogar*, where I would be posted. What might I be able to do in that short week? My Google-able findings alone were heartbreaking: the country was reeling from a violent, thirty-year civil war that had left two hundred thousand dead. Crime was rampant, and my US government was about to sign a contentious trade treaty that would leave the local economy further disenfranchised.

But I knew from my previous trip to Mexico that having thoughtful conversations would at least help me navigate the space more effectively. Throughout the week, my interactions with dozens of the 112 abandoned and abused children living at the hogar made me realize that I was seeing them not as friends and fellow human beings but almost as items on a to-do list, void of identity. I was not yet conditioned to be empathetic, but I was now practicing, and listening throughout this trip helped me move out of my own mindset and away from my own needs and shift to thinking about others' perspectives. Our conversations shed light on the nuances of how a foreigner should and should not become involved in "helping." For example, the orphanage director described well-meaning activists who'd shut down local sweatshops not on par with international labor standards. "What happens when ten sweatshops close? Thirty thousand people lose their jobs, prostitution skyrockets, and more children are left at my doorstep."

Though I had no experience with the immense trauma the children had endured, sexually transmitted infections, rape, and malnourishment, the new empathetic approach I took allowed me to understand their plight in a more detailed context and see how well-intentioned efforts to help could actually make things worse if enacted with a paternalistic sense of *foreigner knows best* rather than with questions about and understanding of a community's needs and preferences. Though I was surrounded by the same tragedies that had left me feeling helpless in Mexico, this time around, my empathetic efforts fueled in me a more purposeful desire to take an action toward a locally requested solution.

As I left Guatemala, I felt a new struggle emerging within me, no longer a concern about understanding what was needed, but about my role in providing support. Of course I wanted to be a superwoman for these children I had grown to care about so deeply in just a week's time. It wasn't good enough for me to board my plane home with far more understanding about the root causes of their suffering. Ultimately, I felt disappointed that no meaningful change had occurred as a result of my being at the *hogar* for one week. *But what did you expect?* I chastised myself. How could I have made any meaningful impact if this was just my one-off spring break adventure while struggle was an everyday reality for these children? Was it not self-centered to think that my transient presence in their lives could have some sort of impact?

At the very least, I reasoned, I should probably temper my ambition with a more reasonable expectation of what my role should be—or even *could* be—in changing a long-standing status quo (likely not the role of a silver bullet). Spending a full semester abroad sounded to me like a good way to test my theory, a solid five months in a country where I could choose one specific issue to address, approach a project with empathy for those I aimed to help, and ideally, do it all with a healthy dose of humility. I chose a program in Accra, Ghana, and within days on the tropical campus, I was already linked up with a local HIV/AIDS clinic. Working with the clinic director, I took on a citywide peer-educator training project for local students who would hone their knowledge about HIV, make promotional posters to combat AIDS-related stigma, and then showcase their artwork at a fund-raising event. In many ways, the semester was a success: I had focused on a specific issue within the major dilemma of global AIDS and didn't become distracted by other needs around me, I was empathetic with local partners upon arrival, and I didn't just parachute in, assuming I had a "right" answer.

Yet I was again left with more questions than answers. Throughout the semester, determined to control the project's success, I stood firmly at the helm of dozens of foreign and local volunteers. I essentially choreographed every moment to shine, and ignored any setback that could have been considered a failure—a local company deciding not to donate or a school choosing not to participate—rather than acknowledge and understand these missed opportunities. I left no room for self-improvement, only for the project progressing forward. Despite my newfound capacity for focus, I became anxious about spending "too long" at any events that weren't work related, afraid they would pull me away from scheduled project plans. Despite my improvements with empathy, I pushed volunteers to work even harder when they felt burnt out, rather than giving them a break.

While these behaviors, in some circumstances, might reflect a valuable tenacity, a quality of single-mindedness common to many of the world's most successful entrepreneurs in general, there was also an indisputable irony and at times an outright harm that resulted from my desire to control every outcome. I lacked humility, a willingness to acknowledge when my actions or reactions were misguided. I immaturely interpreted the word *leader* to mean *controller*, instead of *student* or *partner*.

I carried these lessons in my heart the following summer, when I took a job in Tanzania running an HIV education program similar to the one I worked on in Ghana. When I arrived in the town of Arusha,

I felt like a pro, going through all of the appropriate motions. I had read up on the local culture and politics, learned basic Kiswahili, studied the local HIV epidemic, and spent my first two weeks meeting with local leaders to make sure my online understanding matched up with what was happening on the ground. Eager to avoid my lack of humility in Ghana, I identified a local organization that could codevelop the project; I wanted to be part of a robust team rather than run a one-woman show again. The partnership was a fruitful one, concluding the summer with an HIV Testing Day for local youth, attended by over two thousand students. More than any trip prior, I felt like an amazing everyday ambassador—except for one important detail.

I was still moving a mile a minute and expecting change to happen that quickly too! Rather than being a flexible team leader, I often demonstrated rigid disapproval when partners did not operate according to our planned schedule. In retrospect, I probably ostracized, and maybe even insulted, some of my partners as I imposed my culture's stringent time structure without regard for theirs. Plus, it probably would have been even more instructive to my desire to understand the local environment if I invested more in social downtime, rather than sitting at my laptop, tying up project documents. Though my ambition was rooted in entirely pure, compassionate intentions, I really thought I would make a significant change in a three-month timeline and therefore didn't plan for anything beyond my departure date.

This point hit home, hard, as the project concluded, when my local students called to my attention the flaw in my timeline.

"When are you coming back?" they asked.

I had no answer for them, no answer for myself. I hadn't thought at all about what my involvement would be past the summer, if anything. Skype was still a nascent technology, and only a few of my students had email addresses or regular, reliable internet access.

Would I ever come back to Tanzania? And if not, would the organization be able to carry on this work once I left? I *really* cared. Shouldn't I be more patient with seeing the full issue of HIV/AIDS education through to completion? Or rather, shouldn't I have at least had a more robust exit plan in place—funding resources, scheduled follow-up calls, identification of new mentors—so that the project could continue to run over time, even if I wasn't there?

By the time I arrived in Indonesia a couple years later for a fellowship as a college graduate, I had learned to foresee potential plunges into the disconnectivity paradox, the state of being humanly disconnected even if supremely technologically linked. The more I integrated Everyday Ambassador principles into my professional and personal life, the stronger my relationships became, no matter where I was on the planet. A former classmate in Ghana became a best friend, even though we meet just once every couple years in person. A former student in Tanzania has become like a sister, and thanks to online connection, my friends and family were able to crowd-fund her college education. The disconnectivity paradox, I learned, could only be broken when these precious relationships were prioritized, and then technology was employed to preserve and maintain them. Throughout all these experiences and relationships, I've approached my work in many different countries with awareness and practice of the four values: focus, empathy, humility, and patience. These tools have become more naturally a part of my psyche—though by no means can I operate without needing regular reminders of these precious values.

My life, like most on the planet, has become more digitally involved with every month and year that passes. I become more "connected" with every new app I start using for added convenience and with every new platform I start using, whether to stay in touch with loved ones or engage friends in my work. I know that keeping these four virtues in the forefront of my mind and foundational to my actions will not get any easier. Being an everyday ambassador is likely only going to become even *more* difficult the more wired—and wireless—our lives become. But it's also going to become increasingly more important than ever before.

It has now been over three years since that overcast afternoon in Addis Ababa, when Asfaw and I dined on *njera* and *doro wot*, deeply engaged in feeding each other through conversation and dialogue rather than sitting isolated behind our computers. Although our project resulted in a notable outcome—creating a mobile phone–based patient management system, allowing rural Ethiopian health workers to minimize maternal and child deaths—I feel equally as proud of the deep friendship we forged.

Over the past several years, Asfaw and I persevered throughout a long and at times challenging path toward success, despite frustrating setbacks and obstacles that would have never been overcome without obligation and commitment to each other and our work. We developed a fluent pattern of efficient workflows that included—not overlooked—family updates and personal news. "How is your son doing at medical school?" I asked, aware of how thrilled he was to have Nathaniel follow in his professional footsteps. "How is your grandfather's health?" he inquired, remembering Papou's recent stroke. Practicing this deeper connection illuminates for me the pieces of our cultures, perspectives, and lives that we share with one another, which in turn enriches us professionally and nourishes us personally.

I learned soon after my first lunch meeting with Asfaw about the particular Ethiopian mealtime custom called *gursha*—the practice of *literally* feeding one another. Gursha involves tearing off a soft slab of *njera*, grabbing a portion of *wot*, the size of which is said to be proportional to the amount of affection you hold for someone, and moving that handful of food directly into the beloved person's mouth. This is done before anyone else touches the food on the table, most often by the host to a guest, and constitutes a sign of respect and appreciation. It is a custom I have felt humbled to experience and a norm I like to reciprocate, to signal back my gratitude.

Everyday ambassadorship is, at its core, an exercise in feeding one another, in revolutionizing the idea of service as a two-way street. In our world today, the question is no longer "*Can* we get along?" with people so different from us. Rather, it's "*How* will we get along?" with our diverse global neighbors.

This is a choice you make, *every day*.

What will it be today?

This is, after all, how the world changes: through small, positive exchanges that correct misperceptions and promote peaceful behavior. One-on-one interactions may seem to make a minimal difference, but an impression left on one person or community sends out ripples that influence entire social norms and, eventually, create a new standard of international relations: the grassroots diplomacy that leads to lives being changed for the better.

CONCLUSION

Gone are the days when you and I could sit at home, unaware of events unfolding outside of our hometowns. As I pen this conclusion, social media and our inevitable interconnectedness make it impossible for me, an American, to avoid wars still raging across the Middle East in Israel, Gaza, Syria, and Iraq. Anyone with a Facebook or Twitter account knows of an infectious disease rampaging through West Africa. Citizen journalism continues to reveal environmental pollution and political corruption rampant across major metropolitan centers. Police brutality, hate crimes, gun control, and women's rights are overtaking our social media news feeds across the United States.

By opting into the new social norms of social media, we no longer can opt out of having a strong social conscience. And yet the more bombarded we are with the problems of the world, the more paralyzed we feel about doing anything meaningful in response. As the world becomes smaller, our conflicts seem to explode out of our individual control. But it is crucial to remember that you and I can take very meaningful actions in the face of persistent poverty, disease, discrimination, and war. We can take time to focus in on the specifics of these broad issues and learn the detailed histories and root causes of turmoil. We can research multiple perspectives and expose ourselves to a diversity of opinions, so as to understand the full scope of stakeholders in an issue and their different investments in finding a solution (or perpetuating the problem). We can choose roles to play within the bigger picture of relief and social impact, whatever types of interests or skill sets we possess, whether we're issue experts or "just" caring souls. And we can choose to stick with an issue, or a person, over time, even when it becomes an inconvenience to our lives, until we see progress and resolution, even if it takes many small steps to get to a victory.

One of the best parts about our newly digitized world is that, in our efforts to make a difference in the world, we can do *so* much more than state an opinion or emphasize our approval of another's status update. There are endless applications, websites, and online experiences that exist that allow us to learn about divergent viewpoints; translate content from foreign languages to our mother tongues; see life from someone else's eyes; share our art, ideas, and creations with the world; and engage in real-time conversations with people who share our compassion and service instinct. The digital world holds an endless set of resources to transform our good intentions into meaningful actions, and the power to use these tools is always at our fingertips.

Most remarkable, unlike ever before in human history, you and I can make a positive difference in the world, whether that world is overseas or our own backyard. Our compassion and thoughtfulness are no longer geographically constrained to the people immediately in our daily interactions. Digitally-organized activism and advocacy possess the power to galvanize millions of people to affect social change—organizations like Purpose, Avaaz, and Global Citizen. As long as we can use these powers wisely, by making sure our attention to far-off locales enhances, instead of compromises, our capacity to be kind and human to the people immediately around us, then we will find success in our efforts to change the world for the better.

What will you do to make a difference in a disconnected world? My hope is that in reading this book, you have come to your own customized answer. In reading about various tech traps and their potential solutions, I hope you have come to feel empowered, capable, and inspired to forge authentic, thoughtful human connections and make a difference in someone's life, *today*. In reading about other everyday ambassadors, I hope you have come to a conclusion similar to the one that I did after many years of conversation and camaraderie with people all over the planet: Namely that technology does not fix things; you and I fix things (sometimes with technology). Technology does not connect us; you and I choose to be connected (often via technology). Technology does not diminish the world's inequalities; you and I get out there every day and diminish them (often using technology to tackle these complex issues).

Just as we all have our own unique talents and individual strengths, we all have a cause, a community, a culture, or even a single person for whom we serve as an ambassador. For some of us, a particular social issue, medical disease, or policy problem will determine the course of our ambassadorship, while for others it might be attention to an overall geographic area, a group of people, or even an individual. On some issues, and in some communities, we might find that we're in good company, with many people who stand beside our work and an abundance of shared opinions. In other cases, we might find ourselves solo, like many of the everyday ambassadors in this book, who were pioneering with their ideas and actions, starting a new organization, traveling around the world, being kind to a passenger, or bringing joy to someone in the hospital. These diverse examples were woven together for an important reason: to show that you can start a successful movement, even if you're just a movement of one for now. If you feel inspired to make a difference in someone's life, I hope this book will serve you well in both reflecting on your role in creative positive changes, and in taking meaningful actions to condition yourself as a thoughtful, strategic, humanly-connected changemaker.

Bottom line, the power to make a difference in the world is in our hands. It has always been in our hands, yet too often we give credit, or blame, to technology instead of ourselves. Technology is undoubtedly a powerful tool in our toolboxes, and what distinguishes someone as an everyday ambassador—someone making a positive difference in the world through human connection—is the ability to know when technology is appropriate and when it's getting in the way. It's the person with discipline to not become distracted due to multitasking, with vision to see a multitude of perspectives in an often polarizing environment, with maturity to always stay teachable, and with tenacity to see long-term even in a world that moves at such a rapid pace.

The world needs you—yes, you—right now. And you are more equipped than others ever before in human history to know that a problem exists, hear a multitude of perspectives on a solution, and engage in an action that will make a positive difference. So pass this book along and get out there, whether you're operating in your own household or town, in a new neighborhood or state, or in a different country or continent altogether. Get out there, every day, and pay attention to the people who are around you. In the smallest of ways, find a way to make someone's day better and be a more thoughtful neighbor. In your biggest dreams, find and commit to solving one piece of our global puzzle; identify one measurable part of the solution, and stick with it—for good.

You know that you have the tools it takes to make a difference. Now the choice is yours to get out there and do it.

ACKNOWLEDGMENTS

Everyday Ambassador is my attempt to capture the wisdom of countless teachers and influencers I have been privileged to meet throughout my travels and service work, from my small hometown to the far reaches of the planet. I am grateful, every day, to be a student of so many remarkable teachers.

I am particularly indebted to my Everyday Ambassador teammates, whose hard work and unflagging dedication have built our website into a network for twenty-first-century social change, rendering actionable the concepts presented in this book. To Meg, Audrey, Anya, Kim, Victoria, MacKenzie, Anjana, Morgan, Wendy, Chex, Jennifer, Ananda, and Michael: thank you for your devotion and brilliance.

My gratitude extends as well to lifelong friends and generous mentors I've met in the world of social impact and social change, including my communities at NYU, the Catherine B. Reynolds Program in Social Entrepreneurship, the Academy of Achievement, the Harry S.

Truman Scholarship Foundation, and the Luce Scholars Program. You have granted me unconditional support and countless opportunities to turn my service instincts into action. Thank you.

To Coleen O'Shea, my exceptionally wise and supportive agent: thank you for being my guiding light and for believing in me and sticking by me since day one. To Anna Noak, Gretchen Stelter, and Lindsay Brown, my dedicated and immensely talented editors: thank you for being role models of every EA value as you guided me through this process with consistent grace and patience. I am grateful to the entire Beyond Words family. To my writing circle angels, Magogodi and Tylea: thank you for your consistent, tough-love feedback and reliable sisterhood.

And of course, I send my deepest thanks and appreciation to my loving family—especially Mom, Dad, Matthew, Diana, Andrew, Dee Dee, Yiayia, and Papou, for encouraging my every crazy adventure; to my mum and guru Leigh Blake for your endless support and inspiration; and to the many mentors who have encouraged me not only to look outward and expand my horizons as a global citizen, but also to look within and be intentional and thoughtful about self-development. To my remarkable friends and soul siblings, thank you for your unwavering positivity, generous caretaking, and for sticking with me through every up and down of this journey.

And to the ever-growing Everyday Ambassador family—to everyone whose support and partnership has transformed a small idea into a global social movement—I thank you, and I look forward to continuing this journey together!

EXPLORING EVERYDAY AMBASSADOR QUALITIES FURTHER

In their own words, here are some outstanding examples of everyday ambassadors (EA) in action. Insightful testimonies like these are posted regularly on our website EverydayAmbassador.org, as part of our Wednesday Wisdom blog series. Our contributing writers are individuals who volunteer with EA Partner organizations, sharing their journeys in service and travel that have helped to shape their perspectives on global citizenship and human connection. We welcome you to contribute your stories as well! Whether you work as an everyday ambassador with an organization or as an independent individual, if you have had an experience of human connection through serving others, we would love to hear about it. As you will read in the following profiles, everyday ambassadorship crosses boundaries of location, generation, and vocation—truly, anyone, in any locale, with any set of skills has the potential to participate in everyday ambassadorship.

ANDREA MOORE AND PAVEL REPPO

Cofounders of EA Partner
the Wayfaring Band

Andrea is an artist and entrepreneur who uses writing, performance, and photography to foster connection and dialogue across social and cultural lines. Pavel has been involved with the special needs community since 2006, and finds magic working with young people in particular.

At the Wayfaring Band, we pride ourselves on our values and best practices. We enact a culture of belonging and focus on true and radical inclusion. These values are built upon our model of mutual aid. They are our treasure map that has never led us astray.

Each value has a best practice to ensure that we carry out more abstract principles as well, such as inclusivity. By opening our hands and hearts, we are able to create a more inclusive space.

We value mutual aid, and we practice that by being of service to others, like the time Peter, a man who experiences Down syndrome, traveled to New York City to volunteer in the Hurricane Sandy relief effort, helping with cleaning, supply delivery, and restocking.

Lending a hand to people in need empowers us to ask for help when we need it. A culture of mutual aid enables everyone to be a contributing and valued member of society. We all have special gifts, and we all have special needs, and when we successfully express both, we feel appreciated. Though we are diverse in experience, we are similar in spirit and value each person's contribution.

We value inclusivity. We practice that by showing hospitality to others, like the time we hosted an art show for Sophie and Cody, two young adults who experience special needs. Sophie uses pastels to create vibrant and saturated drawings and also creates wireframe pen drawings. Cody is an author and has shared his story in a zine called *It's Hard to Be Me in My DNA*. Although he never learned how to read or write, he dictated his story, and we transcribed it and tried to indicate his intonation, grammar, pauses, and so on.

Welcoming people with open arms and hearts creates a warm, inclusive space in which everyone can experience an authentic sense of belonging.

We value agency, and we practice that by encouraging reflection, like the time Sean, on top of a soapbox in Cooper Creek Square in Winter Park, Colorado, shared his dreams of going to Hollywood.

In order to know if we are truly self-advocating to the best of our ability, it is important to frequently reflect and take stock of our progress. We wish to empower everyone to make his or her own choices and act from self-knowledge. Wayfaring Band encourages independence and autonomy. Self-awareness helps us face our perceived limitations and exceed our personal expectations, growing in our ability to self-advocate and provide self-care.

We value love, and we practice that by constantly expressing our gratitude, like the time we convened at the end of our Glen Eyrie Castle tour and led an appreciation circle, where everyone says or shows something they appreciate about every band member.

We believe that happiness is directly proportional to the amount of gratitude we carry in our hearts, and we are grateful to all the people, organizations, and opportunities that have supported us on our individual journeys. A person's capacity to give and receive love is a powerful and precious gift, and we cultivate an environment of positivity and confidence where our love can grow and flourish.

We value adventure, and we practice that by encouraging risk taking, like the time we took eleven young adults experiencing special needs on a hot air balloon ride in Albuquerque, New Mexico, or the time we went surfing in Sayulita, Mexico.

When we risk getting out of our comfort zone, we are guaranteed to be exposed to new activities, conversations, connections, and interactions with each other and the world. Our common passion for adventure aligns us, and we nurture this spirit of exploration in our programming and in each other.

SYDNI HERON

A Fellow with EA Partner
Organization Global Citizen Year

Sydni, who hails from Ames, Iowa, spent part of her gap year as a nurse's assistant at a small health clinic in Ecuador. She is passionate about healthcare and writing, and utilized these interests to forge deep human connections with her patients and neighbors in Pichincha.

Patronato is an agency of social character, created to provide social protection to the most vulnerable groups of the *canton* (city neighborhood). The action part of the policies laid down by the Cantonal Government Puerto Quito are to strengthen prevention and treatment projects in health, improve the quality of education, and promote human development, social welfare, and equity to achieve better quality of life for the population.

Thirty to forty patients cycle through El Centro Medico Del Patronato Municipal, a small health clinic in Puerto Quito, Pichincha, Ecuador, each day.

I am a nursing assistant, which puts me on the bottom of the medical food chain. With the exception of emergencies and procedures, patients only see me for a brief period of time prior to their consultation. In those few minutes, I try to give my brightest *¡Buenos días!* and politest *Levántense aquí sin zapatos, por favor*, but I know my smile will do little more than make one annoying part of a typical consultation (the gathering of height, weight, and blood pressure measurements) a little less annoying.

There is one patient, though, I have been working with since I came here three months ago. Her name will remain anonymous to protect patient confidentiality.

She is an older woman. Her fragile and wrinkled skin tells me that. She is reasonably tall for an Ecuadorian but short to an American. Her legs and arms are very thin, but she holds extra weight in a bulging belly—a sign of malnutrition.

Her skin is a light brown but now is painted with darker brown age spots. Oftentimes—most times—when she comes into the clinic, she is dirty.

She is missing two of her front teeth. She always wears a baseball cap. A loose shirt. A colorful skirt that falls to her ankles. On one foot, she wears an old, tattered sandal, and on the other, she wears a once-white bandage now stained brown from dirt.

This patient has diabetes. She developed an ulcer (skin sore) on a portion of her left foot, which led to the necessity to amputate the middle toe and surrounding area of that foot.

I clean and rebandage her foot each day. I have for the last few months.

Had I heard this woman's story from the United States, I would have pitied her. I would have imagined her life hard and her courage brave. I would, though, have imagined her unhappy. How could she achieve happiness—a state of well-being and contentment—with so much weighing her down?

I am not just hearing her story, though. I am learning about it through her own words, her own eyes, and her own ideas. *I am liv-*

ing in it. I hope, through my assistance to patronato, I am playing a strengthening role in it.

When I say that, it is easy to assume I know her life story—how exactly she got to this point, what probably caused her diabetes, and maybe how exactly poor she really is. Through our conversations and her records, I have seen glimpses of all of this, but I *do not think that is where her story lies.*

She loves *telenovelas* (Spanish-language soap operas). Sometimes we put one on in the waiting room just for her as she waits for a mototaxi to pick her up. She likes horses. She doesn't like cloudy days. She has strong faith that there is a God and that he has blessed her very much. (Every time someone praises her healing foot, she says it is all thanks to God.) She has a loving daughter who takes her to the clinic every day, without fail. She smiles a lot.

She seems happy.

I respect her. I admire her. I look forward to seeing how she is each day she comes into the clinic. And I am embarrassed that at one time in my life I would have felt sorrow for her—looked down on her when, now, I so often find myself looking up at her.

Having lived in a "Third World country" for three months, the most important thing I have learned about poverty is that the people I am trying to help do not need my pity—my sympathetic sorrow for those suffering, distressed, or unhappy. If they need anything from me (and I stress the word *if*), it is my time, my care, and my equal treatment.

ANDREW FRANKEL

A Former Group Leader for EA Partner Organization Thinking Beyond Borders

Andrew is currently a program manager at a high school for ethnic minority students in remote western China. After studying Buddhist philosophy at Columbia University, Andrew served Thinking Beyond Borders as a group leader, and has continued to develop a sharp perspective on the appropriate role of foreigners in volunteering abroad.

If you are interested in or connected to the arenas of international development, travel, or service work, you are probably aware of the hackneyed mantras of volunteering abroad and "making a difference" and the subsequent fad of blogging about the evils of voluntourism—the opprobrious title applied by those who know better than shallow and selfish "service work." But postvoluntourist writers only scratch the surface of long-extant questions. They've elided the complexities of these issues, portrayed an oversimplified version of good and evil social engagement, and staked out an uncontestable moral high ground. Disagreeing with them means outing yourself as unworldly, callow, or—yes, trump card!—imperial.

Most problematic is not that these writers tirelessly present some ribbon-tied, bite-sized anecdote: "I used to be young and ignorant and look how I've changed!" It is that they are so ridiculously sanctimonious. They don't see that the high road they insist on taking leads away from the students they're hoping to reach.

What they usually fail to mention is that the more immersed you get, the less certain your motivation and moral convictions become. And the more doubt and prospects of futility wrack your mind. When I was eighteen, I couldn't spell *insolvency*—never mind know what it was—but if I hadn't traveled abroad prior to going to college, I never would have made it such a focus of my studies. Even after studying abroad and graduating, I was clueless. I went to Asia for the first time and trekked and studied and made local friends and volunteered. And even then, I was clueless. Then I got a graduate degree and taught for a student-travel organization, working and studying across the world. And even then, I was clueless. And now I've been living in Asia for eighteen months, am conversant in the local language, have good contacts, spend sixty hours a week providing a desired and necessary service, and even now, I am still virtually clueless.

Antivoluntourists cut off dialogue with students and short-circuit a learning process—as if the goals and means were perfectly obvious. My personal experience as a student-travel leader has made me wary of this rhetoric. A preoccupation with controlling students' behavior can manifest in a disdain for critical learning and resentment for students who don't fit your criteria. New travelers should be allowed to forge their own path—just as we were—and not be written off because they are not yet doctors or engineers with highly applicable skill sets. Are we expecting full-grown Muhammad Yunuses to emerge from third-period algebra?

In the surfeit of articles deriding voluntourism, there is a dearth of better suggestions. It's almost as if everyone wants the cargo-shorts-wearing camera clickers to stay home—reminiscent of how we denigrate places for being touristy because other tourists remind us that we are too. Nothing shatters our pride faster than seeing another dweeb as obtrusive as we are!

But what's the alternative—for these inquisitive young thinkers to stay home because they're not yet qualified? (And if that happens, we won't get them back when they are qualified.) Is the only alternative to being a voluntourist simply not to go at all? Wouldn't we then complain that the youth are uncultured and ignorant on global issues? If you are never a level-one tourist, you never move on to level two. How can anyone criticize these kids when we were there not too long ago and—let's face it, world savers—might still be there today.

A realistic alternative to the reflections of the antivoluntourists is a critical approach that places further resources and responsibility in the hands of our students, and the best example of an organization that embodies this pedagogy is Thinking Beyond Borders. This innovative organization not only engages deeply with issues and approaches international development humbly, it understands that personal development takes time, and you can only meet students where they are. A core principle of the program is that if everyone comes willing to learn in an environment of humility and inquiry, students are far more open to questioning and improving their own assumptions and habits. And still, we stood in front of the Taj Mahal, making peace signs and taking pictures. Who didn't their first time there?

When we as leaders are more concerned with acknowledging faults than creating a dialogue about why there's dissonance, we miss valuable opportunities for improvement—both for the students and ourselves. Whether you want to reference Plato's Cave or Shantideva's description of the bodhisattva ideal, the point is the same: seeing through the illusions isn't the vocation of teachers or scholars—returning to the cave, reseeing the misperceptions, and working with others as we collectively retrace and redefine our awareness is the essence of education.

We all need to see more accurately the situations we encounter and our impact on our hosts. From a wider perspective, I agree with many of the observations and rebukes of the antivoluntourists and would probably take them even further, but I can't understand the usefulness of an opinion that impairs rather than incites students' desire to participate in their own education. When applying our justifiably strict codes of conduct to working abroad, let's start with ourselves and not those looking to us for leadership: it's important to remember that we were once students, and we still are—or at least we should be.

SOPHY JAMES

A Teacher at the Shanti Bhavan Children's Project through EA Partner Organization Omprakash

Sophy recently graduated from the elementary education program at Florida State University and deeply believes that education holds the power to completely change the world. Shanti Bhavan has given her the chance to put her passion for providing equal education for all individuals, regardless of economic means, into action.

The announcement to my family that I wanted to travel to rural India three weeks after my college graduation was met with many reactions, including surprise, skepticism, and contempt. My middle-class, suburban family could not seem to comprehend why I would not continue on my current path of the "American dream." Why push against the social norm when I had a perfectly comfortable life laid out for me? According to my family, the next logical step would be to get a good job that had decent health insurance and a 401(k) plan in a safe, suburban school in the heartland of America. For them, spending an extended period of time volunteering at a nonprofit in a developing nation was unfathomable.

My family's reactions immediately made me second-guess my intentions to volunteer. More than anyone else they only wanted the best for me, only wanted me to be happy. If they thought it was such a radically terrible idea, maybe I was missing the bigger picture of what I should be aiming for in my life. They had given me every chance to succeed; I wanted my postcollege endeavors to continue to make them proud. However, the more I sat and thought about it, the more I came to realize that my parents had given me every opportunity in order to ensure that I was successful. The fact that I had never created an opportunity for myself, but instead had always waited for others to present them to me, made my decision. I would be traveling to rural India without my parents' support—emotionally or financially.

I journeyed to South India feeling very alone. I arrived at the Shanti Bhavan Children's Project located in rural Tamil Nadu, India, with a lot to prove not only to myself but also to everyone who was against my plan from the beginning. Shanti Bhavan is both an English school and a home for children from India's *dalit*, or untouchable caste. The school provides seventeen years of intense intervention for its students. Shanti Bhavan hopes that its students will graduate from university and become successful professionals within their chosen fields—and eventually help to transform the communities into which they were born.

Currently, my day begins at 6:30 AM, helping the ninth- and eleventh-grade students understand the daily world news that they will then present to the entire school. I spend most of my day in the second-grade classroom, where I have gained a tremendous amount of valuable teaching experience.

"Show me your ASDF monster claws on the keyboard."

"Quiet hands raised if you know which number is the tens place."

"Who can tell me a sentence in which we use an exclamation point?"

Throughout the day, so much time is spent doing not assigned but, rather, assumed tasks. I treasure the moments helping an outrageously nervous eleventh-grade girl prep for her public speaking performance and reading to the kindergartners in their dorm as they rapidly fall asleep after a long day of work and play.

The students at Shanti Bhavan have taught me so much more than I will ever be able to teach them. I have learned how to speak more eloquently, work with extremely limited resources, and dedicate myself completely to one single task at a time. I have learned to become a harsh critic of myself, because that is the only way to improve. Put simply, this experience has helped transform me into a more well-rounded individual and educator. Dr. Abraham George, the founder of Shanti Bhavan, believes that "compassion without action is nothing, while compassion with action is everything." I would like to think that I have always held compassion, but Shanti Bhavan has given me an outlet to turn this compassion into action.

My parents are finally coming around. This past week, my father said to me, "You are going through such a metaphysical metamorphosis, and we could not be more proud of you." Before India, I seriously doubted that I could do anything completely independently without help from my family. Now, I have found my independence, and I realize that the only person who knows what is best for you is you. Going against social norms and into the unknown is difficult, but this experience has given me more insight into myself and the world around me than a lifetime of work in the United States could have ever done.

GABRIELA GUERRERO

A Volunteer with EA Partner Organization America's Unofficial Ambassadors

Gabriela is a student of studio art at San Francisco State University (SFSU). She volunteered in Tajikistan at the Tajik State University of Commerce (TSUC) with America's Unofficial Ambassadors.

This trip I spent months preparing for has come to an end. It's my last night in Dushanbe. I've contributed what I could to my placement at Tajik State University of Commerce and tried my best to make a lasting and positive impact. I didn't go into this with any expectations, and I think that helped make the experience more fulfilling. I received some advice from America's Unoffical Ambassadors Program Coordinator Stefan Cornibert that this would be a learn-as-you-go type of experience. A part of me liked that nothing was too concrete. Allowing for flexibility provided Noureen, my incredible teaching partner at the university, and me with opportunities to represent both our country and its beliefs while opening up the floor to the Tajik perspective.

For example, because our students were within our same age group, we could comfortably discuss similarities and differences on topics ranging from class schedules to gay marriage to the pros and cons of international volunteerism. A prompt that Noureen and I gave to our students went along the lines of how they felt having volunteers come from America and whether they saw it as a positive experience. Sabrina, an English student at the university, responded by saying:

> I see volunteerism as a positive experience because we learn a lot about the English language, culture, and communication from the volunteers. Volunteerism is good for countries because it consolidates friendships between them. We are very glad to see our foreign friends in Tajikistan, and we are very glad to work with them. It helps us to improve our language, listening, and speaking skills as well as our outlook and also helps us for our going abroad. It's my dream to visit America once in my life, so I try to learn English because it's necessary for me and volunteerism helps us with it.

There were several agree-to-disagree moments—like when a student of mine blatantly said that women could not lead a country—but regardless, it was exhilarating to be able to have these types of conversations without creating an offensive environment.

As far as long-term impacts, I was able to translate the university website, as well as two university brochures, into proper English. Sometimes this portion of my schedule was stressful, given the occasional language barrier, but there was always a way to reach a mutual understanding. Otherwise, I'd just laugh it off when there was simply no way to translate a certain word from Russian into English. Furthermore, the process encouraged a cultural exchange about education systems. I had an interesting conversation with two students about how they take eleven courses per semester, whereas I take only five. Though such vast differences between TSUC and SFSU were apparent, this did not imply any real separation between us.

Staying in Dushanbe for the amount of time I did, although it was about two weeks shorter than the rest of the volunteers, gave enough time for me to grow accustomed to their way of life. It's been a beautiful adjustment. Leaving the country showed me how much value is put on the fact that I was born and raised in California. I was confronted with weird questions like, "So, do you know Tom Cruise?" But, I too had naïve questions in mind, like when I invited a friend to lunch on the second day of Ramadan! To a certain extent, it hurt to realize how much of the world I am unaware of, but on the other hand, I couldn't be more thankful to have settled in a foreign-living environment.

STEPHANIE SANDERS

Program Coordinator for EA Partner Organization
S.O.U.L. Foundation in Uganda

Stephanie has worked for S.O.U.L. Foundation since 2012, helping to manage their various programs in Uganda, Bujagali Falls community, such as education, food security, women's empowerment, and health initiatives.

Lovina pointed and paced furiously.

Her voice raised to a level so much louder than any Ugandan I had heard that suddenly her five-foot stature felt intimidating. She needed supplies for her chicken farm, and I was the project manager responsible for providing these supplies. As the Ugandan field coordinators, Oko and Phoebe, rushed to translate her words, I scrambled to put the pieces together. But my presence, and attempts to help, seemed only to add to her agitation.

Before I knew it, Oko was asking me to just walk away from the situation. I felt lost, confused, and frustrated that I wasn't being given a fair chance to work things out. Lovina seemed to hate me, or maybe just the idea of me, and I couldn't help but feel responsible. What had I gotten myself into?

I was only three weeks into my new position with S.O.U.L. Foundation, based in a village in southern Uganda. My initial interest in S.O.U.L. came from a deep respect for its organizational mission: to be a grassroots community organization that creates sustainable economic solutions through programs for women's empowerment, food security, health, and education.

Lovina's chicken rearing was part of a microenterprise initiative in our women's empowerment program. S.O.U.L. teaches women like Lovina all sorts of skills, like keeping financial records, managing a bank account, and marketing, and even provides an initial investment so that after a few successful sales cycles, the organization can step aside and let women run their businesses independently.

I realized that getting on the right track with Lovina had less to do with a business relationship—which my organization clearly was providing—and more to do with a personal relationship. I decided to visit her program group, Group D, almost daily to start forming closer, more meaningful bonds with group members.

Over the next seven months I worked hard and often felt that my commitment was being tested. But the more time I spent with Lovina and her twelve peers, the more I felt invested in their successes. Slowly, the harshness of our first encounter began to dissipate.

When we had chicken markets, which required mornings as early as 2:00 AM, I made it a priority to slaughter with Group D. I couldn't join in much conversation, but the women sweetly laughed at my attempts to speak Lusoga and were impressed when I uttered new words. We may have lacked formal communication, but we started a bond by working together for a common cause.

Things really happened once I met Lovina's son.

One afternoon, he entered the brooder, and we greeted each other with a smile, his bashful and mine beaming. That day, I happened to have something that locals don't see often—an apple. I generously handed it over, and he quickly said thank you and ran outside.

It's amazing how big a difference a small token can make. Culturally, gifts are signs of friendship, but I was surprised when Lovina greeted me with the most sincere smile. It was a nod of acceptance, and layers of upbringing, culture, and socioeconomic status were stripped away. What was left was connection in its freest form, arising from love and understanding.

Lessons like these I will carry with me for the rest of my life: that even the smallest efforts can lead to change on a much broader scale, that your world can transform when you embrace a new way of thinking, and that when you can't rely on words, actions reveal true intentions. From this experience and so many others in Uganda, I have learned that working without ego gives me the chance to be open to these lessons, because it gives ways for understanding and love to act as driving forces in my work. Though it is easier said than done, on the days when everything seems to be going wrong, these are the sentiments that keep me going.

As the social activist Howard Zinn once said, "Small acts, when multiplied by millions of people, can transform the world." My relationship with Lovina, and so many others in our community, has allowed me to foster and practice the values of patience and understanding that help me focus on the small acts that end up making the biggest difference.

KELLY IMATHIU KANANDO MUTETI

A Fellow with the EA Partner Organization Global Health Corps

Kelly hails from Nairobi, Kenya, having earned his BS in Environmental Health and MPH at Moi University in Eldoret. Prior to his Global Health Corps assignment, Kelly worked with the East African Sexual Health Rights Initiative to support networks of LGBTI and sex workers organizations, and with Hiros Foundation, where he supported women's health rights, non-discrimination of LGBTI persons, and said governance across East Africa.

A lot of times when people hear of the United States, they think of opportunities; it's the land of milk and honey.

Being a Kenyan, born and raised in the coastal regions, I have witnessed what the idea of going to the United States has done to the ears of those who have not had the chance to experience America in its raw form. The stereotypes that have emerged from Africa generally hail America as a place of *haves*.

But living here in the United States for four months now, in an underserved neighborhood of Newark, New Jersey, has changed the way I view my world. Everyone in this corner of the country works hard. Sometimes, they work much harder than Kenyans could even fathom. I see youthful teenage girls walk into the daylight with strollers, searching for a source of employment that will ultimately provide them the shelter and little food to feed four others waiting for them at home.

Living in America has also taught me that we each exist within a movement. A cause which we believe can create community and move mountains, something that probably exceeds passion but springs forth from belief. Health is one of the movements I have strongly come to be a part of. Working with vulnerable populations and witnessing the work of your hands moving spirits is practically the order of my day at Covenant House in Newark. Sharing the call to service with another Global Health Corps fellow at Covenant House, an American, further brings me great perspective on how two nations can work together and how we can create positive synergy through this work.

Covenant House believes in sanctuary. What that means is that we serve with purpose and a mission to motivate homeless young people to step ahead toward making wise decisions and choices. In my role at the organization, I help youth realize that choice is something they possess, something they will always have. However, the consequences of these choices are irreversible.

Innately, my opinion is that this is a universally adopted notion of truth, whether you hail from Newark or Nairobi. I am my accomplishments. For young people at the Covenant House, this means that their achievements as young homeless people will always be theirs, and as young people they will make use of the resources available to them for any next step forward.

So I ask this question again. Is there an American dream? What does it look like? How does a young person with no home experience it? How is it relevant to someone like me, who isn't American?

So far, I see what I consider to be the American dream every day in the strength of the community at Covenant House. Thus, I have come to believe that the American dream, the land of milk and honey, isn't one collective, achievable goal. It is a duty we each take on every day to create and re-create our own definition of our dream in the communities in which we exist.

And most of the time, as in my experience at the Covenant House, it is a dream that is inextricably tied up in someone else's.

LEE STROMAN

Communications and Outreach Coordinator for EA Partner Organization Semilla Nueva

In her position at Semilla Nueva, Lee has worked to amplify the voices of small holder farmers in Guatemala by sharing their stories and concerns with global audiences. Semilla Nueva helps rural Guatemalan farmers find a path to prosperity and health through sustainable agriculture technologies and farmer-to-farmer education.

In 2005, a team of college students armed with goodwill and the best of intentions set off to Nicaragua. Their mission: to build a house for a poor Central American family.

As the last of the nails were hammered in, they stepped back to admire their accomplishments. Neighbors walked over to ask about the house. But as many thank-yous were offered, an equal amount of requests accompanied them. Could they build their family a house, give them a job, or pay their medical bills? One request particularly touched everyone's heart; a man came to work for free, and at the end of the week asked for four hundred dollars to pay for a surgery to save his mother's life. How could so little be necessary to do so much? But a deeper realization came to these eighteen- and nineteen-year-olds—that no one could build enough houses or provide enough free medical services to end poverty. Changes were needed to end the root causes of poverty rather than just alleviate its symptoms.

Fast-forward eight years. It's 2013, and an organization named Semilla Nueva, started by those once naïve boys, is changing the face of rural Guatemala—one farmer at a time. It's simple; the majority of the world's poor are farmers. What they need are ways to increase their incomes from farming. Semilla Nueva, which means new seed, brings them simple farming changes that help them rebuild the soil, feed their families, and up to double their incomes. The organization's aim is to help farmers earn enough to build their own houses and pay their own medical bills.

A perfect way to understand what Semilla Nueva does for farmers is through a local bean called *pigeonpea*. Semilla Nueva is currently working to introduce a new type of pigeonpea that is small enough to be grown in between the rows of farmers' traditional crops, corn and sesame. Farmers don't increase their costs, don't lose their traditional crops, and get an extra crop to eat and sell. Pigeonpea also rebuilds soil and helps farmers grow a complete protein in one of the fourth most malnourished countries in the world. It's a win-win for farmers and an innovation that could help the over 250,000 families who grow corn in tropical Guatemala. Working on the ground, Semilla Nueva's staff has seen the impacts that these changes can make in a farmer's life.

Saul Gonzalez is a farmer in the Guatemalan village of Conrado de la Cruz. He is the sole breadwinner for his family and lately for many of his grandchildren as well. Despite being one of the poorest farmers Semilla Nueva works with, Saul never ceases to amaze and inspire with his contagious smile, unstoppable work ethic, and incessant willingness to try new ideas. He tried pigeonpea on a small parcel of land in 2011 and, seeing the results, planted pigeonpea with all his crops in 2012. And that decision may have saved a life.

Last year, Saul learned that his nine-year-old granddaughter's brain surgery had been unsuccessful. The public hospital had tried to stop the advance of a brain tumor, but it came back, and it was beyond the government doctors' abilities. A local nonprofit teamed up with a hospital in Canada to provide another surgery to Maria, but only if Saul could cover $220 of visa applications and other costs. He asked friends and family, but no one had the money to help.

Saul didn't have the money, and again the dilemma surfaced that is so common in the developing world: a few hundred dollars for someone's life. But Saul did have something. This was the first year he'd planted a large amount of pigeonpea, and it would soon be ready to harvest. He sold the crop in advance and paid the visa.

Maria began her surgery on February 22, 2014, at the children's hospital in Toronto.

Semilla Nueva's hope and pride come from the continual repeat of this story. Farmer by farmer, surgery by surgery, home by home, they are watching as their partner farmers earn the means to care for their own lives. It is a string of stories that are just beginning.

Next year, they plan to watch farmers earn over $25,000 from selling pigeonpea. The year after, they expect six digits. And this is only one of the technologies Semilla Nueva is promoting in their ten partner villages. As other NGOs and government agencies are starting to copy this model, this impact can only grow. More than numbers on a paper, this is what keeps us going. We are seeing these lives change in front of us. Their stories become ours. And the moral of the story is simple: with some dedication and some smarts, we can solve big problems together.

MEG VANDEUSEN

A Member of the EA Team and a Former Volunteer at HOPE Gardens in North Carolina

Meg is a graduate of the University of North Carolina at Chapel Hill where she studied women and gender studies. Her global service work has brought her to East Africa and South Asia, yet her commitment to public service is just as strong in her American communities. Meg is currently serving as a Fulbright scholar to Malaysia.

Nine thirty in the morning on the very first Saturday after starting my undergraduate I rolled out of bed to hop into a car with complete strangers hoping to get my hands a little dirty.

I was heading to HOPE, Homeless Outreach Poverty Eradication, a student organization at the University of North Carolina at Chapel Hill dedicated to fostering relationships with, and exploring innovative solutions for individuals struggling with poverty. The project HOPE Gardens engages participants in sustainable agriculture activities, to bring communities together and address challenges faced in access to healthy food. Although I knew nothing about fruit trees, the leaders trusted me to work with Gary (name changed for privacy), a man who used his employment at the Garden the previous summer to obtain housing, in directing a fraternity volunteer group to weed our orchard.

After just a few weekends of working with Gary and the other volunteers I was hooked. During this time I experienced a moment that, for me, was the epitome of HOPE Gardens.

I had the chance to meet Roger (name changed for privacy), a quiet middle-aged man from the local homeless shelter who rode with me to the garden some weekends. He growled when he talked and had a closed-off demeanor. Slowly, the longer his hands were immersed in the earth, the more he began to ease out of his tough-guy stance. As it turned out, in his heyday, Roger had been a landscaping guru. When we assigned the task of planting pansies to overly energetic elementary schoolers, Roger was not having their disorganized planting pattern.

He knelt down next to a small blond bob of hair. I felt terrified that his gruff voice and calloused hands would scare off the pigtailed seven-year-old. Instead, she looked up at his softened gaze and listened to the simple instructions he offered of first digging a hole before planting. Soon more and more kids crowded around Roger for their planting lessons. Together, Roger and several children filled an entire row of flowers.

It was here I realized my own invisible (and unfair) assumption—I had harbored some underlying fear that Roger would not be able to teach gardening, even though I had no idea how to grow flowers myself! Until that moment, the people I had been working with were merely recipients of the garden's services.

Listening to the children's squeals of delight I began to see something different. The children might have been there for a fun afternoon in the dirt, but they were making the garden their own. Roger might have been there to benefit from HOPE Gardens, but he was also creating a safe space for others to learn. Increasingly,

I, too, began to rely on the relationships I developed with people at the shelter, and my original idea of "serving others" became a much more holistic experience of teamwork and community.

Seeing Roger for who he was allowed me to let go of other assumptions as well. When I became involved in the garden in my second semester, my priority became engaging the mothers at the Women's and Children's shelter who rarely came outdoors with us. My zealous dreams of having a mother and child walk hand-in-hand down the road to harvest produce for their dinner were quickly dampened. Didn't they see that their children were having fun and wanted to be a part of that experience? Couldn't they understand that adding free, fresh vegetables to the frozen pizza dinner would be good for them?

I had assumed the barriers were straightforward, but over time I learned that there are plenty of good, interconnected reasons why women opted not to come join us. Yes, they wanted to participate, but after a long day of working, searching for something better, they did not have the energy to watch their kids when someone else would. Yes, they wanted to take better care of their family's health, but they could not afford to prioritize walking to the garden before dark over feeding their children on time.

Once I understood where the mothers were coming from, once I let go of my presumptive vision of their involvement with the Gardens, I was free to listen to their needs and ideas instead. Together we developed a sustainable, long-term community within the women's shelter through a garden on their own land. We noted an immediate interest for the mothers to eat healthier and help their kids learn to do the same. Instead of us always asking them to come to our garden, we brought produce to them and created opportunities to share cooking, culture, and experiences among each other. Women who did not know the difference between a cucumber and a zucchini started making zucchini fritters for potlucks at the garden, and stubborn children who refused to touch a vegetable would make themselves a sandwich with a 1:10 meat-to-lettuce ratio!

My time at the Gardens has encouraged me to recognize that everyone has some shared experience, even if it is just monotonous shoveling. I have been able to cultivate my love for conversation into the ability to ask for, and share, stories with just about anyone. The stories they tell never cease to astound me. The people I have met through HOPE are some of the strongest that I know, and have the power to create change within their own communities.

However, I have also become acutely aware that this is not so simple for everyone to see. Sometimes I find myself feeling in a more foreign environment trying to educate my classmates and community members on homelessness than I do when I'm hanging out with my friends in the homeless shelters. People continue to equate the face of homelessness to the pan-handler with whom they always try to avoid eye contact. When individuals join HOPE for the first time, they hold an innate fear of not knowing what to say or how to act. I can't provide them with a script, nor do I wish that I could.

What I can offer are my own lessons from the four years I worked and grew within this community, and words of encouragement to seek their own.

First, embrace vulnerability. Members of the homeless community are just as human as you or me. They have experienced an unfortunate life circumstance which, more likely than not, could one day affect us as well. We must be willing to recognize that the language of hope and fear is universal. Unless we are willing to shatter our comfort barrier and share ourselves with a stranger, no one will want to speak that language with us.

Second, believe that you need to engage with people who are different from you in order to grow. Understanding another's life story will allow you to become humbled and begin to work thoughtfully and passionately for a better world.

Finally, believe in yourself. Take a risk and engage in something that allows you to see the human spirit. You will know what to do, how to act, and what to say. You won't be perfect. You will make mistakes. You may offend someone. But, you will be forgiven. Allow yourself to be helped.

Now, go get your hands dirty and build some relationships!

EVERYDAY AMBASSADOR PARTNERS

Everyday Ambassador (EA) is a network of global citizens who believe that human connection, even in an increasingly digital world, is the key to lasting, positive social change. Our vision is a world in which all travelers and volunteers approach the act of crossing borders—whether national, class, race, or otherwise—with attitudes of undistracted focus, empathy, humility, and patience toward diverse people they meet.

Partners within the EA network consist of outstanding organizations and companies who provide people with opportunities, products, and resources that help them live the everyday ambassador vision and lifestyle.

EA Partners are travel, volunteer, and advocacy organizations who can help you get directly involved in a service project or organization, anywhere in the world. Current EA Partners include:

America's Unofficial Ambassadors (AUA): AUA is an organization dedicated to fostering thoughtful citizen diplomacy among young Americans and their counterparts in the Muslim World. AUA sends Americans to communities throughout Africa, Asia, and the Middle East with service assignments in fields like education, human rights, and public health. By serving as English teachers, grant proposal writers, website designers, or health educators, AUA volunteers engage in short-term service trips that are part of larger, long-lasting partnerships that AUA holds with communities. AUA programs are open to university students and graduates, schools and educators, and professionals in other fields. Don't forget to check out AUA's brilliant and robust Directory of Recommended Organizations to search for even more opportunities to be an unofficial ambassador.
unofficialambassadors.com

AquaAid International: AquaAid designs and implements clean water and sanitation projects for communities in rural Nicaragua, believing that there is "no one size fits all development solution." They tailor each project uniquely to specific communities, soliciting advice from local leaders as well as engagement from children and students who help design creative education programs about sanitation and hygiene.
aquaaid-international.org

Foundation for Sustainable Development (FSD): FSD provides international exchange opportunities in Africa, Asia, and Latin America, in which volunteers can engage in thoughtful and respectful projects with community-based partners. FSD's projects are guided by principles of ensuring community-ownership, strengthening existing assets within local communities, creating long-lasting impact, and forging partnerships based on trust, respect, and effi-

cacy. You can apply to travel and serve with FSD anywhere from one week to a full year.
fsdinternational.org

Global Citizen: Global Citizen is a global advocacy organization that engages everyday people in the mission to end extreme poverty by 2030. Through their innovative and highly-accessible online platform, members can take action by accessing up-to-date information, linking up with service organizations, and participating in events and campaigns that strive to end injustice and inequality in the world.
globalcitizen.org

Global Citizen Year (GCY): GCY is a social enterprise that offers "bridge year" opportunities to graduating high school seniors, a year engaged in a service project abroad before starting college. GCY believes in the principles of total immersion, requiring participants to commit at least 9 months and learn the local language of their new community, and the longevity of lessons learned during the experience, which are designed to prepare students for success well beyond their time abroad.
globalcitizenyear.org

Global Health Corps (GHC): GHC pairs up young professionals from the US and from nations abroad to tackle a health system reform issue on a paid, year-long fellowship. By placing these pairs at partner organizations based across Africa and within the US, GHC's program is designed to foster cross-cultural communication and understanding. Although the focus of projects are in the health sector, Fellows contribute skill-sets ranging from technology and computer science to education, business development, and impact evaluation research.
ghcorps.org

Learning Service: LS is an organization dedicated to reforming the international volunteering environment from one of service learning into "learning service"—meaning that we must first learn about a community and an issue before we can aspire to provide help. This movement for learning equips young travelers, particularly those on their first trips abroad, with the skills and mindsets needed to be genuinely helpful, not unintentionally harmful, to the communities they aim to serve.
learningservice.info

Omprakash Foundation: Omprakash builds bridges between aspiring volunteers and grassroots social impact organizations all over the world by curating educational global volunteer experiences that focus on building meaningful, strong relationships. In addition to focusing on forging trust and honesty between volunteers and communities, Omprakash also cares deeply about creating affordable and accessible opportunities for young people, and their database can link you to over one hundred fifty pre-vetted Partner organizations from over thirty countries, free of charge.
omprakash.org

Semilla Nueva: Semilla Nueva helps farmers in rural Guatemala to create and benefit from agricultural education programs that increase farmers' incomes, crop yield, and, ultimately, local food security, particularly for the rural poor. By integrating new sustainable agriculture technologies into collaborative projects with community organizations and local government offices, Semilla Nueva shows how to build respectful, responsible, and effective partnerships across borders.
semillanueva.org

S.O.U.L. Foundation: S.O.U.L. Foundation is a non-profit organization dedicated to supporting the Bujagali Falls community of Uganda

with a variety of health, education, and economic empowerment initiatives. S.O.U.L. specializes in engaging donors and volunteers with very little exposure to Ugandan culture in meaningful community-led development initiatives, that emphasize the power of strong cross-cultural communication.
souluganda.org

Blue Bridge Project: Blue Bridge Project is a volunteer abroad program exclusively for high school students, designed to immerse students at a young age in global development issues through hands-on projects and guided reflection exercises.
bluebridgeproject.com

The Wayfaring Band: The Wayfaring Band is an organization dedicated to the philosophy of "mutual aid"—that in every act of service we offer to others, we are equally the recipients of positive change as well. The Band designs and runs a series of road trips, social programs, and leadership trainings for young adults who experience special needs and emerging thought leaders.
thewayfaringband.com

Thinking Beyond Borders (TBB): TBB is an educational nonprofit organization that provides volunteer opportunities—entire gap years as well as tailored gap semesters—to young adults who aspire to make a difference on critical global issues. TBB's programs are designed based on the latest research about international education and social change leadership, and aim to equip participants with skills that will enable them to be global citizens for a lifetime.
thinkingbeyondborders.org

TulaLens: TulaLens partners with NGOs, social enterprises, and companies that serve the poor to create products and services that

are better designed to meet the needs of their beneficiaries. Using simple mobile phone technologies, they solicit and utilize feedback, and offer services to their low-income customers no matter their mobile carrier, language, or literacy level.
tulalens.org

Use Your Difference (UYD) Magazine: UYD Magazine is a lifestyle magazine founded on the concept of "using your difference to make a difference," encouraging young people who are "different"—those who have grown up surrounded by more than one culture or in more than one country, also called, "Third Culture kids"—to share their stories and perspectives in order to educate audiences, build bridges, and minimize misunderstandings.
uydmag.com

Beyond our formal partnerships, EA also endorses the following programs:

AFS Intercultural Program: Volunteer with AFS in one of fifty countries; it's open to teenagers, young adults, and teachers seeking an intercultural experience abroad. The AFS network of support is impressive—a strong community of people dedicated to creating a two-way exchange.
afs.org

AmeriCorps: Each year, AmeriCorps offers seventy-five thousand opportunities for adults of all ages and backgrounds to serve within a network of local and national nonprofit groups throughout the United States. Remember: you can be an ambassador in your own country! It's about crossing comfort zones.
nationalservice.gov/programs/americorps

Child Family Health International: CFHI runs global service-learning programs for medical and other health science students that focus on cultural competency in the health setting.
cfhi.org

City Year: If you're an urban American, you've likely seen the corps members' signature red jackets. At City Year's twenty-five locations across the United States, diverse teams of young people serve full-time in schools for eleven months, working to improve student attendance, behavior, and course performance in English and math.
cityyear.org

The Experiment in International Living (EIL): Founded in 1932, EIL is so longstanding that the Peace Corps based its program on this concept! EIL offers three-to-five-week summer volunteer programs in more than twenty countries around the world, open to students who have completed their ninth, tenth, eleventh, or twelfth grade year but have not yet entered college or university. In order to go to French- or Spanish-speaking countries, language study is a requirement.
experiment.org

Gap Medics: Gap Medics offers high quality health sector volunteer internships to pre-medical students or new physicians interested in shadowing opportunities overseas, with incredible attention to each volunteer's experience.
gapmedics.com

Global Volunteer Network: "Connecting people with communities in need" through international volunteer placements, this program is for individuals interested in promoting local solutions to local problems.
globalvolunteernetwork.org

The Henry Luce Foundation Scholars Program: Sights set on Asia? This excellent program provides stipends, language training, and individualized professional placement in Asia for fifteen to eighteen Luce Scholars each year and welcomes applications from college seniors, graduate students, and young professionals in a variety of fields who have had limited exposure to Asia.
www.hluce.org/lsprogram.aspx

Peace Corps: Unlike other programs positioned entirely to "help others," Peace Corps volunteers provide technical assistance and aim to "promote a better understanding of Americans on the part of the peoples served"—and vice versa.
peacecorps.gov

Purpose: Purpose is an organization dedicated to "movement entrepreneurship"—the creation and nurturing of innovative social change organizations and campaigns that cultivate mass participation in concrete change objectives. Steeped in the values of common humanity, mass participation, and pragmatic idealism, Purpose is your home base for information, resources, and updates on becoming meaningfully engaged in social change campaigns.
purpose.com

Spark MicroGrants: Spark MicroGrants proactively reaches out to under-resourced communities who are isolated from traditional aid. Spark offers them an opportunity to do their own development projects, transforming beneficiaries into change makers and developing new youth leaders in the developing world.
sparkmicrogrants.org

Teach for America and Teach for All: Teach for America recruits, trains, and develops dedicated recent US college graduates of all

backgrounds to teach for two years in urban and rural public schools. Based on the Teach for America model, the global off-shoot Teach for All is designed to cultivate leadership in the world of education reform, and ensure every child on the planet has access to a high quality education.
teachforamerica.org
teachforall.org/en

United World Colleges (UWC): For teens and young adults looking for an alternative to traditional high school and college experiences—try UWC! UWC schools "deliver a challenging and transformative educational experience to a diverse cross section of students, inspiring them to create a more peaceful and sustainable future."
uwc.org

How to Become a Partner

EA Partners are organizations that uphold the EA mission: to create a cultural shift in the world of travel and volunteerism/service so that good intentions are always translated into respectful social change efforts.

Are you interested in your organization being certified as an EA Partner? If the following criteria apply, contact kate@everydayambassador.org to register.

- My organization believes that, in a world where we're more digitally connected than ever before, we're all too often less humanly connected. We do not let social media and digital devices get in the way of real-life conversations; rather we train our travelers/volunteers/participants in skills of interpersonal interaction.
- My organization focuses on cultivating strong relationships with the people we aim to serve.

- My organization rejects terminology, like saving or helping others, and instead we phrase our service in terms of two-way exchanges and mutual growth.
- My organization promotes principles of focus, empathy, humility, and patience and a culture of self-awareness and cultural sensitivity.

Once an EA Partner, your organization will be eligible for a feature article in the Wednesday Wisdom blog series. In this series, we feature stories from participants in organizations like yours, to illustrate what the front lines of everyday ambassador training looks like all around the world.

HOW TO BECOME PART OF THE EVERYDAY AMBASSADOR COMMUNITY

I hope you will decide to remain a part of the global community of Everyday Ambassadors after having read this book! There are many ways you can get involved, at whatever level of commitment you are comfortable giving.

Stay in Touch

Subscribe to our blog at everydayambassador.org. You can also link up with us on several social media sites. (Remember, technology's not evil, but use the tools wisely—don't refresh EA's Twitter feed while you're spending time with loved ones!)

- **Facebook:** facebook.com/everydayambassador
- **Twitter:** @everydayAMB
- **Instagram:** instagram.com/everydayambassador
- **Pinterest:** pinterest.com/everydayamb
- **LinkedIn:** linkedin.com/company/everyday-ambassador

We also love to hear about other service-oriented networks and other organizations raising the bar on what it means to engage in world-changing work, so reach out and let us know of any that you support!

Share Your Personal Experiences

We warmly invite you to submit a piece of writing to our blog. Here are the guidelines for submitting a piece of writing to EA for publication:

1. **What gets published on EA?**
   Everyday Ambassador highlights the power of everyday people to create immensely positive change in the world. By *change*, we don't mean ending hunger, fighting poverty, or universalizing health and education. Positive change in the world means building strong relationships—with everyone, including the people you aim to serve. Why? Because with relationships come trust, respect, and dignity. Hearts and minds change. Eventually, behavior and actions change and a better world emerges. Everyday Ambassador is dedicated to sharing your lessons and showcasing the relationships that make your service work so meaningful.

2. **What should I write about?**
   Guest blog posts should be between five hundred and eight hundred words and focus on (1) the obstacles you have encountered when it comes to human connection across borders (national, ethnic, religious, socioeconomic, age, gender, and so on), and (2) the strategies you have learned to employ in your service work to truly connect on a human level when it comes to achieving social impact. Organizations may submit posts addressing the same points but from an institutional perspective.

3. **What voice or writing style should I use?**
   Your post should feature raw feelings, doubts, concerns, and instincts, but be sure to approach each piece from the view of a mentor. We are not interested in pleasant-sounding answers to complex problems of global struggle; we are interested in hearing your honest, poignant, even troubling teaching moments and the questions they prompt in your heart. Human interest stories get clicks, and clicks can help establish a new culture, so be sure to write at a human level, minimizing jargon and technical language. Don't be afraid to be controversial!

4. **How do I submit a post for publication?**
   Submit posts to Audrey del Rosario at audrey@everydayambassador.org, with the subject line: EA Post for Review [Your Name]. Please include three to five photos, as well as any video links that you would like to include in the post. Posts will be reviewed and scheduled for publication, and you will be contacted in advance of publication to review any edits to the post. If you are submitting a piece as part of a larger campaign or advocacy effort, please be specific about your date preferences for publication. We will always do our best to accommodate.

Host an EA Workshop

To link up with Everyday Ambassador offline and promote EA principles at your campus or workplace, set up a training or workshop with EA on any the following topics:

- Constructive uses of technology and the nature of social media today
- Cultural awareness in a volunteer or travel setting

- Meaningful ways to serve a community and to become an everyday ambassador
- Personal growth from service and travel
- Voluntourism and the nature of service abroad
- Reflection after completing a travel or service opportunity

Interested in hosting an Everyday Ambassador event or workshop? Contact Kate Otto at kate@everydayambassador.org.

Join the EA Team

We're a team of volunteers who manage the website and our global network, and we're always happy to have new hands on deck. If you are interested in joining the Everyday Ambassador team, please contact Kate Otto at kate@everydayambassador.org.

NOTES

1: The Disconnectivity Paradox

1. International Telecommunication Union, "The World in 2014: ICT Facts and Figures," April 2014, itu.int/en/ITU-D/Statistics/Documents/facts/ICTFactsFigures2014-e.pdf.
2. Aaron Smith, "Smartphone Ownership 2013," Pew Research Internet Project, June 5, 2013, pewinternet.org/2013/06/05/smartphone-ownership-2013.
3. Pew Research Center, "Social Networking Fact Sheet," Pew Research Internet Project, January 2014, pewinternet.org/fact-sheets/social-networking-fact-sheet.
4. Gwenn Schurgin O'Keeffe and Kathleen Clarke-Pearson, "The Impact of Social Media on Children, Adolescents, and Families," *Pediatrics* 127 (2011): 800–804. doi: 10.1542/peds.2011-0054.
5. Janna Anderson and Lee Rainie, "Digital Life in 2025," Pew Research Internet Project, March 11, 2014, pewinternet.org/2014/03/11/digital-life-in-2025.
6. Mark Kingwell, "Beyond the Book," *Harper's Magazine*, August 2013: 15, harpers.org/archive/2013/08/beyond-the-book.

7. Ryan Hamilton, Kathleen Vohs, Anne-Laure Sellier, and Tom Meyvis, "Being of Two Minds: Switching Mindsets Exhausts Self-Regulatory Resources," *Organizational Behavior and Human Decision Processes* (2010): last accessed September 12, 2014, http://ssrn.com/abstract=1147689.

2: What Is an Everyday Ambassador?

1. "Maya Angelou Quotes," ThinkExist.com, http://thinkexist.com/quotation/i-ve_learned_that_people_will_forget_what_you/341107.html, accessed December 1, 2014.

3: Focus: Windows Open, Doors Close

1. John M. Grohol, "FOMO Addiction: The Fear of Missing Out," *World of Psychology* (blog), PsychCentral, last accessed September 12, 2014, psychcentral.com/blog/archives/2011/04/14/fomo-addiction-the-fear-of-missing-out.
2. Katrina Schwartz, "Age of Distraction: Why It's Crucial for Students to Learn to Focus," *Mind/Shift* (blog), December 5, 2013, blogs.kqed.org/mindshift/2013/12/age-of-distraction-why-its-crucial-for-students-to-learn-to-focus.
3. Aimee Cunningham, "Kids' Self-Control Is Crucial for Their Future Success," *Scientific American*, June 23, 2011, scientificamerican.com/article/where-theres-a-will.
4. Martin Hilbert and Priscila López, "The World's Technological Capacity to Store, Communicate, and Compute Information," *Science* 332 (2011): 60–65. doi: 10.1126/science.1200970.

4: Empathy: Avoiding Digital Divisiveness

1. M. D. Conover, "Political Polarization on Twitter." Paper presented at the Fifth International AAAI Conference on Weblogs and Social Media, Barcelona, Spain, July 17–21, 2011.
2. Sarita Yardi and Danah Boyd, "Dynamic Debates: An Analysis of Group Polarization Over Time on Twitter," *Bulletin of Science Technology Society* 30 (2010): 316–327. doi: 10.1177/0270467610380011.
3. Greater Good: The Science of a Meaningful Life, "What Is Empathy?" accessed June 28, 2014, greatergood.berkeley.edu/topic/empathy/definition.
4. Samuel P. Oliner and Pearl Oliner, *Altruistic Personality: Rescuers of Jews in Nazi Europe* (New York: Touchstone, 1992).

5. B. A. Scott, J. A. Colquitt, Elizabeth Layne Paddock, and T. A. Judge, "A Daily Investigation of the Role of Manager Empathy on Employee Well-Being," *Organizational Behavior and Human Decision Processes* 113, no. 2 (2012): 127–140. Research Collection Lee Kong Chian School of Business. ink.library.smu.edu.sg/cgi/viewcontent.cgi?article=3964&context=lkcsb_research.
6. Courage to Care home page, last modified 2014, courage2care.net.
7. G. Steffgen, A. Konig, J. Pfetsch, and A. Melzer, "Are Cyberbullies Less Empathic? Adolescents' Cyberbullying Behavior and Empathic Responsiveness," *Cyberpsychology, Behavior, and Social Networking* 14 (November 2011): 643–648. doi: 10.1089/cyber.2010.0445.
8. Gabrielle Blanquart and David M. Cook, "Twitter Influence and Cumulative Perceptions of Extremist Support: A Case Study of Geert Wilders," in the Proceedings of the 4th Australian Counter Terrorism Conference (Perth, Australia: Edith Cowan University, 2013), 7, http://ro.ecu.edu.au/cgi/viewcontent.cgi? article=1021&context=act.
9. Ines von Behr, Anaïs Reding, Charlie Edwards, and Luke Gribbon, "Radicalisation in the Digital Era: The Use of the Internet in 15 Cases of Terrorism and Extremism," *RAND Corporation Europe* (2013).
10. David Lubell, "Welcoming Immigrants: Why Empathy Is Smart Economics for Cities," *Forbes*, July 10, 2014, forbes.com/sites/ashoka/2014/07/10/welcoming-immigrants-why-empathy-is-smart-economics-for-cities.
11. Kathleen Toner, "Creating an Oasis in Southern 'Food Desert,'" CNN Heroes, October 21, 2013, cnn.com/2013/09/12/living/cnnheroes-emmons-food-deserts.

5: Humility: The Un-Google-able Insight

1. R. Eric Landrum, "Measuring Dispositional Humility: A First Approximation," *Psychological Reports* 108 (2011): 217–228, sspa.boisestate.edu/psychology/files/2011/03/Measuring-dispositional-humility-A-first-approximation-Landrum-2011.pdf.
2. Maia Szalavitz, "Humility: A Quiet, Underappreciated Strength," *Time*, April 27, 2012, healthland.time.com/2012/04/27/humility-a-quiet-underappreciated-strength.
3. Jordan Paul LaBouff, Wade C. Rowatt, Megan K. Johnson, Jo-Ann Tsang, and Grace McCullough Willerton, "Humble Persons Are More Helpful than Less Humble Persons: Evidence from Three Studies," *The Journal of Positive Psychology* 7 (December 2011): 16–29. doi: 10.1080/17439760.2011.626787.

6: Patience: High Speed Is Not High Impact

1. Louis C.K., "Everything's Amazing, and Nobody's Happy," YouTube video, 4:11, posted by Matt Bedard, January 4, 2014, youtube.com /watch?v=uEY58fiSK8E.
2. Pew Research Center, "The Impact of Digital Tools on Student Writing and How Writing Is Taught in Schools," Pew Research Internet Project, July 16, 2013, pewinternet.org/2013/07/16/the-impact-of-digital-tools-on-student-writing-and-how-writing-is-taught-in-schools-2.
3. Judith Orloff, *Emotional Freedom: Liberate Yourself from Negative Emotions and Transform Your Life* (New York: Three Rivers Press, 2011).
4. Narayan Janakiraman, Robert J. Meyer, and Stephen J. Hooch, "The Psychology of Decisions to Abandon Waits for Service," *Journal of Marketing Research*, 2011.
5. Kent Nerburn, *Make Me an Instrument of Your Peace* (New York: HarperOne, 1999), 60.
6. Ibid, 61.

SPECIAL THANKS

I would like to give a very special thanks to all the everyday ambassadors featured in this book, and the many whom I have met and interviewed over the past few years who are not in this book by name, but whose spirit and example shine through the words on these pages. Thank you for generously sharing your time and experiences with me, and for being the living proof of everyday ambassadorship that inspired me to write this book.

Miriam Altman
Mark Arnoldy
Sonia Chokshi
Rebecca Corey
Cesar Francia
Conor French
Uraidah Hassani
Nadi Kaonga
Akhila Kolisetty
Hannah Lane
Jennifer Lentfer
Eric Lu
Toni Maraviglia
Laura McNulty
Patrick Meier
Prentice Onayemi
Benjamin Orbach
Julia Rozier
Zim Ugochukwu
Weh Yeoh